A FEW KIND WORDS

"*Encounter God* is a beautiful invitation to slow down and recognize the divine fingerprints in everyday life. With gentle wisdom and grace, Arlene Mancilla Cook draws readers into sacred reflection, reminding us that God is not only present in our mountaintop moments but also in the quiet, ordinary spaces we often overlook. Each story, prayer, and reflection opens a door to deeper intimacy with the One who loves us beyond measure. This book is not meant to be rushed—it's meant to be savored, prayed through, and experienced. A true companion for anyone longing to feel God's presence more deeply in their daily walk."

SUSAN NEAL, RN, MBA, MHS
Award-winning author of *12 Ways to Age Gracefully*

"With lyrical wisdom and compassionate honesty, Arlene Mancilla Cook offers an invitation to experience God's presence in the quiet, unpolished corners of life. Each page is a reminder that growth in grace is not about doing more; it's about resting more deeply in the One who holds every moment. Arlene writes with a tenderness that feels like a conversation with a trusted friend.

"This book is a gentle reminder that grace meets us not in our striving, but in our surrender. *Encounter God: When Ordinary Moments Reveal Extraordinary Love* invites you to slow down, breathe deeply, and see how God's love is woven into the everyday chapters of your story. A soul-soothing journey into the heart of grace. Arlene's words remind us that God's beauty often blooms in the most ordinary places."

BISHOP GERALD DOGGETT
Doggett Leadership Institute

"In this beautifully crafted devotional, Arlene invites readers to join her on a transformative journey into the very HEART of God. With vivid storytelling, thoughtful biblical insight, and reflective questions, she guides us toward a deeper, more personal understanding of God's character and presence. Her warm, relational approach not only enriches our spiritual perspective but also encourages meaningful connection with God in our daily lives. If you're seeking a devotional that cultivates intimacy with God and inspires genuine spiritual growth, this is it!"

KAREN M. THACKER, PHD
Licensed Professional Counselor, Adjunct Professor at the
Townsend Institute-Concordia University Irvine, author of
Surviving the Scarlet Letter and *The Journey Forward Workbook:
Daily Steps to Achieve Emotional Balance & Healthier Relationships*

ENCOUNTER GOD

Encounter God

When Ordinary Moments Reveal Extraordinary Love

ARLENE MANCILLA COOK

TJP

TRANSFORMATION
—JOURNEY—
PUBLISHING

Melbourne, Florida

Encounter God: When Ordinary Moments Reveal Extraordinary Love

Copyright © 2026 Arlene Mancilla Cook

All rights reserved. No portion of this book may be reproduced, distributed, or transmitted in any form—including electronic, mechanical, photocopying, or recording—without prior written consent from the author, except for brief passages quoted in reviews or critical analysis.

Published by Transformation Journey Publishing, Melbourne, Florida

Cover and Interior Photos by Arlene Mancilla Cook, www.arlenecook.com and iStock.com/PhanuwatNandee

Cover and Interior Design by Imagine!® Studios, www.ArtsImagine.com

Scripture quotations marked AMP taken from the Amplified® Bible (AMP), Copyright © 2015 by The Lockman Foundation. Scripture quotations marked AMPC taken from the Amplified® Bible (AMPC), Copyright © 1954, 1958, 1962, 1964, 1965, 1987 by The Lockman Foundation. Scripture quotations marked NASB taken from the (NASB®) New American Standard Bible®, Copyright © 1960, 1971, 1977, 1995, 2020 by The Lockman Foundation. Scripture quotations marked NASB1995 taken from the New American Standard Bible®, Copyright © 1960, 1971, 1977, 1995 by The Lockman Foundation. Used by permission. www.Lockman.org

Scripture quotations marked KJV are taken from the KING JAMES VERSION, public domain.

Scripture quotations marked MSG are taken from The Message, copyright © 1993, 2002, 2018 by Eugene H. Peterson. Used by permission of NavPress. All rights reserved. Represented by Tyndale House Publishers.

Scripture quotations marked NIV taken from The Holy Bible, New International Version®, NIV®. Copyright © 1973, 1978, 1984, 2011 by Biblica, Inc. Scripture quotations marked NIrV taken from The Holy Bible, New International Reader's Version®, NIrV® Copyright © 1995, 1996, 1998, 2014 by Biblica, Inc. Used with permission of Zondervan. www.zondervan.com

Scripture quotations marked TPT are from The Passion Translation®. Copyright © 2017, 2018, 2020 by Passion & Fire Ministries, Inc. Used by permission. All rights reserved. ThePassionTranslation.com.

Scripture quotations marked The Voice taken from The Voice™. Copyright © 2012 by Ecclesia Bible Society. Used by permission. All rights reserved.

AI Training Prohibition: This work may not be used to train artificial intelligence systems or machine learning models without the author's explicit written permission. All rights to license this content for AI development purposes are reserved by the author.

ISBN: 979-8-9947332-0-2 (paperback)
ISBN: 979-8-9947332-1-9 (e-book)

Library of Congress Control Number: 2026904379

First printing: March 2026

To my ABBA, Who created me, designed me, and delights in me.

To Jesus, Who proved His boundless love at the highest price.

*To the Holy Spirit, Who whispers inspiration
and heals my deepest wounds.*

*And to my husband, who smiles knowingly
when I say, "I have an idea . . .";
you are my balance, my support, my home.*

TABLE OF CONTENTS

FOREWORD

Some books inform, and others invite. This one invites. It calls you, not with thunder or spectacle, but with the quiet, steady voice that speaks in the middle of an ordinary Tuesday. Arlene Mancilla Cook has crafted a work that feels less like reading and more like remembering. Remembering how close God has always been, how tenderly love has always pursued you, and how heaven often hides in the smallest, simplest moments.

In these pages, Arlene does something rare. She brings the divine down from the clouds and places His presence into the rhythms of everyday life. Into the conversations we overlook, the interruptions we resent, and the emotions we'd rather avoid. With honesty and warmth, she shows us that encountering God isn't reserved for mountaintops or miracles; it is woven into the fabric of our daily steps. Her stories and reflections illuminate a truth many of us forget. God is not distant. He is here, revealing His extraordinary love in ways subtle enough to miss but powerful enough to change everything.

What makes this book especially compelling is Arlene herself. She writes not as a lecturer but as a fellow traveler. One who has wrestled, wondered, laughed, grieved, and, through it all, discovered a God who is intimately involved in every detail. Her voice is gentle yet confident, vulnerable yet grounded in faith. She offers not formulas but insights, not perfection but presence. In doing so, she creates a safe place for readers to explore their own encounters with the divine.

Whether you are seeking reassurance, renewal, or simply a reminder that God still speaks, this book will meet you where you are. It will widen your vision. It will soften your heart. And, perhaps most beautifully, it will help you recognize the holy in the humblest of moments.

May these pages open your eyes to the extraordinary love already surrounding you. May you find yourself surprised, again and again, by the God who reveals Himself in the midst of your daily life. And may Arlene's words inspire you to notice, to listen, and to believe that every moment, no matter how ordinary, has the potential to become an encounter with Him.

Bishop Gerald Doggett
Doggett Leadership Institute

ACKNOWLEDGMENTS

They say it takes a village, and I'm blessed to have been raised by one that still holds me up today.

To Papi and Mami—whose courageous sacrifices and boundless love gave me wings. Your faith has lit a path that I pray will shine through every generation to come. You left everything behind and came to this beautiful country with just a few suitcases and hearts full of dreams for me and my siblings. You gave up everything so we could have more. You didn't just talk about a better life, you built it. You not only taught me how to dream big, how to take risks, how to reach for the stars, and how to never, ever give up. You modeled it. Everything I am, every brave thing I've ever done, started with watching you do the bravest thing of all.

To my brother Pompey—you were the first in my family to read my words and marvel at them. Those emails you wrote me? I still have them. You made me believe my writing was out of this world, and that kind of gift? You can't put a price on it.

Nicky, my twin soul, sometimes we need people who believe in us louder than our own doubts—you've had more confidence in what I could do than I've ever had in myself.

Gloria, my sister-mother, you've loved me, nurtured me, and rescued me more than once—from the time I was a baby to this very moment. You showed me what it means to be held.

Mirta, these last few years you've carried what I couldn't—caring for Mom with love and dedication. Because of you, I had the time to discover this passion for writing.

To my children, my heart walking outside my body—watching you grow into the women of God who serve Him daily and raise your children in His ways, is a dream come true. It's the fulfillment of every prayer I didn't even know how to pray. You are everything I hoped for and so much more.

And to my grandchildren, my daily dose of joy and entertainment—you bring smiles I didn't know I had in me. You cross my mind all day long, warming my heart and reminding me to laugh at life.

To my Encounter family, you listened to countless messages, encouraging me to be confident and sitting with me through every revelation and rough delivery.

To my closest friends—you spent hours reading what I wrote, encouraged me through the doubt, and believed in me when belief felt impossible. That's a priceless gift, and I don't take it lightly.

And finally, to those who appear in these stories. You were God's instruments to teach me lessons about love I couldn't have learned any other way. Thank you for being part of my journey, even when it was hard.

This book exists because I don't walk alone. I never have.

A NOTE BEFORE YOU BEGIN

The pages you're about to read carry pieces of my story—some tender, some raw, all shared with the hope that they might meet you in your own journey. These reflections are not written to accuse, expose, or cast blame. They are offered as windows into moments that shaped me, in case they help illuminate something in you.

Throughout this book, you'll encounter personal experiences, including stories involving my family—especially my parents. I want to say clearly and with deep conviction: my intention is never to dishonor them. Quite the opposite. My parents, whom I mention in several stories, did the best they could under the circumstances we lived in—the stress and struggles of an immigrant family navigating unfamiliar terrain. They faced language barriers and cultural values that often clashed with their own—a kind of emotional and relational strain that happens when two worlds collide and you're trying to raise children in one while holding onto the heart of another. That tension is sometimes called cultural dissonance, and it shaped many of our experiences.

Still, my parents made countless sacrifices so that we, their children, might have a better life. They have my respect, my honor, and my grace—for giving us more than I saw many parents give. I ask that you extend that grace to them as well.

Some stories may stir memories, wounds, or long-buried emotions. If that happens, be gentle with yourself and reach out—to a friend, counselor, or trusted community. God designed us to heal in relationship, with Him and with one another. You are not alone.

This book is not just mine—it's yours too, if you choose to enter it. May it be a companion, a mirror, and a gentle guide toward restoration.

AN INVITATION TO GRACE-PACED GROWTH

Your spiritual journey is not a race with a finish line—it's a conversation with a God who meets you in every season, every mood, every moment of readiness or weariness.

These pages hold stories of ordinary moments where heaven touched earth, where broken pieces were made beautiful, where whispered prayers were tenderly answered. But more than stories, they hold space for your own heart to breathe and respond as it's able.

Some days you'll arrive here with energy for deep soul-searching, ready to excavate old wounds and plant new seeds of healing. Other days you'll come exhausted, needing only the gentle reminder that you are seen, known, and cherished just as you are. Every arrival is welcome here.

Read lightly when life feels heavy. Let the stories be medicine for a weary spirit.

Reflect gently when your heart has room. Choose the questions that whisper your name, leaving the rest for another day. The first two questions in the reflection section are the lighter ones.

Dive deeply when your soul is ready. Questions 3–6 at the end of each chapter invite you into deep waters. Drift into them when your heart has the capacity to process more, integrating new understanding. But remember—spiritual growth blooms in its own season, not under the pressure of forced timelines.

God doesn't check His watch when you come to Him. He doesn't sigh with impatience when you need to move slowly. His love doesn't diminish when you can only manage small steps.

This is your invitation to grace-paced growth—where the only requirement is showing up as you are, taking what you need, and trusting that God's gentle hands are writing something beautiful with the chapters of your story.

A LETTER TO THE READER

I want you to know I was thinking about you the whole time I was writing. I know, you're probably saying—you don't even know me. But even though that might be true, I saw you: the one who needs to know you're not alone, the one reaching for a hand to move forward. And I saw you too—the one who's simply curious about what this walk with God looks like.

For so many years, I hid my struggles, because like so many other people, I thought they were unique. My ache was different. My longings didn't make sense. Until I started searching. And in my searching I found books. Books written by people who read my mail. Writers who seemed to see me and could bring clarity to my pain, my confusion, even the things I thought were just me. I realized my struggles were unique yet universal. My pain was different but similar to yours. And one day I knew I needed to be brave, not just for me but for you. Because I wanted you to know—you are not alone. I wanted you to know you could make it to the other side—because after so many years, I did.

In all honesty, I'm a very private person. But I knew I needed to choose vulnerability, to share my stories and the lessons I learned. If I could clear the path, like a bulldozer pushing through the scrubs, maybe you could find your way home too.

As you read my stories, you may find they reflect pieces of yours—my pain echoing your own, my joy awakening joy you'd forgotten was there. That's because God made each one of us unique but very much the same. I wrote this in hopes that in reading my stories, you would discover yours. And more than all of that, I wrote this because I want you to know you've got a constant Companion

Who whispers your name, Whose fingerprints appear in the daily journey of your life and Who finds pleasure in your company.

The reflection questions at the end of each chapter are designed to help you notice patterns and identify feelings. If you find that answering the questions is awakening parts of your story you hadn't realized was there, I know what that feels like. That's your spirit longing for growth, that's your soul tasting clarity. If you feel emotions that are new or deeper, that's your heart coming alive—it's the taste of freedom. This is when you make the choice to take the journey. The journey to more, to a fuller life. But take your time. Give yourself grace. It's a hike. You may find yourself out of breath, but then you'll realize the air is cleaner. Stop and breathe it in. Then keep going.

If at any time it feels like too much, remember the journey of life was never meant to be taken alone. As you'll read in my stories, much of my healing came through imperfect humans. Find someone who knows the journey and who is ahead of you—and ask for help. A friend, a counselor, a pastor. Someone more experienced, or with training, to walk with you. It'll be worth it.

My goal in writing this is to encourage you to reach higher, heal deeper, and laugh harder. But the greatest reason for my writing is so that you could experience "how wide and long and high and deep is the love of Christ"—for you! I'm excited! Ready? Let's go!

O my soul, come, praise the Eternal;
sing a song from a grateful heart;
sing and never forget all the good He has done.
Despite all your many offenses, He forgives and releases you.
More than any doctor, He heals your diseases.
He reaches deep into the pit to deliver you from death.
He crowns you with unfailing love and compassion
like a king.
When your soul is famished and withering,
He fills you with good and beautiful things, satisfying
you as long as you live.
He makes you strong like an eagle, restoring your youth.

PSALM 103:2–5 (THE VOICE)

THE HEART OF THE JOURNEY

Years ago, God gave me a promise from Isaiah 61:1 (AMP)—

"He has sent me to bind up [the wounds of] the brokenhearted, to proclaim release [from confinement and condemnation] to the [physical and spiritual] captives."

That verse became more than words on a page. That verse became my lifeline. I held onto it for my own freedom, through every dark season, every moment I wondered if wholeness was possible. And it came true. My heart was healed. My captivity ended. I found my way home.

Now I'm holding onto that same promise for you.

It's become my calling, the reason I do what I do, and the heartbeat behind every story in this book.

I organized these 31 stories around the word HEART—because this is about your heart coming alive, just like mine did. These aren't steps to check off or stages to complete in order. They're more like different windows into the same beautiful reality—what happens when God restores a heart. You might experience all five in a single moment, or spend months in just one section. There's no timeline, no pressure, no right way to do this.

H—Hearing God's Voice
Learning to recognize the many ways He speaks

E—Experiencing God's Love
Encountering who He truly is

- His heart revealed directly to you,
- His heart reflected through others

A—Aligning with God's Truth
Replacing lies with the truth that sets you free

R—Reclaiming God's Design
Rediscovering who you were always meant to be

T—Trusting God's Plan
Learning to let go and rest in His faithfulness

As you read, you'll discover what a restored heart looks like—one that can hear Him, receive His love, believe His truth, become who He created, and trust where He's leading.

If it happened for me, I know it can happen for you.

SECTION I

HEARING GOD'S VOICE is about awakening to the sacred whispers woven through your everyday moments. About learning to listen to the quiet nudges and unexpected redirections. When your heart learns to listen, you'll discover He's been speaking all along.

I

My Image of God

Every prayer you whisper, every failure you face, and every step of your spiritual journey is shaped by the image of God you hold in your heart. But what if a single sentence could shatter the false deity you've constructed from childhood wounds and reveal the true countenance of Love—the One who has been waiting for you all along?

> *As he passed in front of Moses, he called out. He said, "I am the LORD, the LORD. I am the God who is tender and kind. I am gracious. I am slow to get angry. I am faithful and full of love"*
>
> EXODUS 34:6 (NIRV)

"God isn't standing over you with a hammer waiting for you to do something wrong." My friend Mary's eyes widened as she spoke.

Her words caught me off guard, leaving me utterly speechless. My pulse raced, and my face flushed, betraying the fear and shame

> "God isn't standing over you with a hammer waiting for you to do something wrong."

I tried to hide. Overwhelmed and dizzy, I stood frozen, unable to react.

But what she said also deeply resonated in my heart. Her words landed with force, etching themselves into my being and imprinting my mind with a truth that, at the time, seemed distant and foreign. Even now, after three decades, I can hear them as if they were spoken moments ago.

Mary's attempt to realign my misconception about God came during a trying season in my life and marriage, marked by unprecedented challenges. The sounds of love songs and wedding bells had faded behind us. The weight of our wedding bands felt reassuring, giving us a naïve confidence that we were ready to face adulthood. Carrying a three-month-old in our arms, the appeal of independence pulled us away from our hometown and our first home. We moved from a modern condominium with all the amenities in the city to unfamiliar territory in a much smaller town.

Disregarding our parents' warnings about moving proved costly, impacting our marriage and my once carefree spirit. After a few years, the vibrant, fun-loving personality I once radiated in high school seemed elusive and subdued. Now, adulting and independence felt overrated. In many ways I felt lost. Trying to navigate this new life without the support of my mother, my family, and the church I had been a part of was much harder than I anticipated. Clouds of depression hovered over me, and my sense of humor had all but disappeared. I felt myself withdrawing. With each day, I became more reserved, my timid and sensitive nature emerging as I tried to make sense of everything shifting around me.

After several failed friendships in our new town, I realized I needed a relationship with someone willing to be honest with me. Eventually, I found Mary. While her friendship had been my saving grace, her words at times painted stark realities and truths I didn't feel ready to process. As a result, I often felt my defenses building, battling the urge to withdraw, even though my heart longed for connection.

This inner conflict was at work when Mary's words washed over me—first like a splash of ice-cold water thrown in my face. Then like a soothing balm, gently nurturing the child within, who yearned for her father's unconditional love.

The assurance that God was not angry at me despite my inadequacies and shortcomings felt like experiencing a secret dream I'd never dared think might come true. Yet it also peeled back layers of denial, exposing the hidden impact of my earthly father's anger, urging me to confront a concealed pain so that I could embrace the warmth of my heavenly Father's love.

Negative self-talk began to swirl in my head. *I've been a Christian for several years now, how could I have missed this truth? I should have seen this myself!* The perfectionism I lived with daily reared its head again and feelings of guilt and shame made me want to run away from my friend.

Being raised in a rigid religion that stressed the importance of living by the *Ten Commandments* caused me to place a tremendous emphasis on performance. In addition, the discipline I saw was firm and unforgiving. I learned early on to walk carefully, afraid of what might happen if I messed up. The more perfectly I behaved, the more I could avoid the kind of punishment I dreaded.

When my friend corrected me, offering an image of a gentle God instead of the harsh judge I'd imagined, it felt like an assault on my carefully guarded, perfectionistic identity. Realizing someone could see my flawed thinking left me feeling naked and ashamed.

However, I came to see that her words revealed something deeper than my imperfections. They exposed my true picture of God.

As children, we see our parents and caregivers through tinted glasses. These influence the way we perceive God, affecting how we relate to Him. To heal our perception of our Heavenly Father, we need to recognize and remove these lenses so we can see Him as He truly is. When Mary told me God wasn't waiting to hammer me, it made me question. *Did I see God as a harsh overlord, eager to pounce on me for my mistakes, ready to condemn me?*

At that moment, I conjured up an image of God, His eyebrows furrowed, staring down at me with His eyes full of anger.

> As children, we see our parents and caregivers through tinted glasses. These influence the way we perceive God, affecting how we relate to Him.

Suddenly, another image appeared in my mind's eye—that of my earthly father. Although he never physically harmed me, my father lived in a state of continuous stress, stayed emotionally distant, and found it difficult to connect with me. His social persona, marked by humor and laughter, contrasted with his stern, intimidating figure at home. In our household, fear and respect were synonymous—and fear him, we did.

A rapid succession of mental snapshots from my past made me pause and ponder. *Was my perception of God filtered through and shaped by my knowledge of my father?* I now realized it was. Despite my years in a relationship with God, my mind thought His love and acceptance of me was based on my ability to do everything perfectly. But it wasn't God who imposed this belief on me. It was the picture of my father that I had superimposed over my picture of God!

Although I caught fleeting glimpses of grace through the years, I had been conditioned to believe that God's love and acceptance was based on my ability to please Him. This made it difficult for me to experience God's devotion and adoration when I felt flawed or made mistakes.

Realizing this set me on a quest that would forever change how I saw God, ultimately transforming my relationship with Him. I became driven to dive into the Scriptures, to explore what the Bible actually said about this God that I feared. *Who are You, God? And what are You really like?* I wanted to know. I soon discovered that even the Old Testament, with its seemingly stern judgments, overflows with His unconditional, tender-hearted, nurturing love.

It's fascinating to witness the different ways God uses to communicate with us sometimes. One sentence spoken by a friend can radically shift our perspective. God used Mary's words to completely reshape my thinking, removing a heavy blanket of blame, guilt, and shame. He replaced it with a weightless mantle of love and joy.

As I immersed myself in the Bible, my understanding of God began to change. The Scriptures came alive, and I saw examples of His great love for me everywhere, bringing me to tears. It was as though God Himself was highlighting verses, eagerly revealing His true character to me.

I began to recognize the blessings in my life. I began to see how much He loved me and the more I saw that, the more I loved Him. The more I loved Him, the closer I drew to Him. And the closer I drew to Him, the more I was willing to allow the Holy Spirit to convict me of my faults. Yet, in the conviction I felt no condemnation. It was about learning and growing and knowing that He loved me despite my flaws and imperfection. I was forgiven.

It was a process, but little by little, I began to welcome correction and embrace change. For the first time in my life, I understood that God's discipline is always enveloped in kindness and love. When I come before Him, I can expect to receive "love, love, and more love." This same beautiful embrace of love and acceptance is waiting for you.

"I've never quit loving you and never will. Expect love, love, and more love!"

JEREMIAH 31:3 (MSG)

Father,

I come to You with an open heart, recognizing that the image I've carried of You may be clouded by shadows from my past. Gently remove the lenses that distort how I see Your face—those layers of fear, performance, and conditional love that I've mistakenly attributed to You. Show me who You truly are, not as I've imagined or feared You to be.

When I stumble and fall—and I will—give me the courage to run toward You rather than away. Let me feel the truth that Your arms open wider when I'm broken, not when I'm perfect. Plant this reality so deeply within me that it transforms how I pray, how I fail, and how I receive Your love.

I've spent so much time trying to earn what You've always freely given. As I read Your words, help me see Your heart—the tenderness I've missed. Let what's true replace what I've believed about You for so long. When You redirect me, remind me it comes from love, not from a God who's keeping score.

Reintroduce Yourself to me, Lord—not as the God I've feared, but as the Father who has been waiting, with endless patience, for me to discover who You've been all along. Amen.

A Moment of Reflection

1. *What Scripture passages have most shaped your understanding of God's character?*

____

____

____

____

2. *Where do you see evidence of God's tender love in your life that challenges your old image of Him?*

____

____

____

____

3. *Do you hesitate to bring certain requests to God? Are there parts of yourself you hide from Him out of fear or shame?*

____

____

____

____

4. *Take a moment to picture God looking at you. What's His expression? How have past relationships with authority figures shaped this image?*

____

____

____

____

5. *When you make a mistake or fall into sin, what is your first instinct? Do you run toward God or away from Him?*

____

____

____

____

6. *Think about a time when you received correction from someone. How might your reaction reflect your deeper beliefs about God's discipline?*

____

____

____

____

2

When Silence Speaks and God Listens

Do your prayers seem to vanish into thin air, met with cosmic silence? Think again. God's not just listening—He's catching every whispered sigh your heart makes before it even reaches your lips.

> **Behold, the Lord's hand is not so short that it cannot save,**
> **Nor His ear so impaired that it cannot hear.**
>
> ISAIAH 59:1 (AMP)

"Oh. So, what you are saying is that God actually has ears?" The professor's voice cut through the classroom, dripping with sarcasm. His eyebrows arched as he scanned the room, waiting for someone to challenge him.

"God can have ears. After all, He is God." The words left my mouth before I could second-guess myself. The professor's

11

momentary silence felt like victory—small, but significant.

This confrontation happened during my second year of college in a World Religions course. As someone deeply invested in understanding people, my goal in enrolling had been to learn about diverse faiths, seeking to engage more meaningfully with those from different backgrounds. Although my belief in Jesus Christ was unwavering, deeply rooted in eight years of Catholic schooling and a personal relationship with Him, I held respect for the paths others were taking in their quest for truth. But now I found myself doubting my decision. The professor's cold, ridiculing sarcasm was not what I had signed up for.

> God's not just listening—He's catching every whispered sigh your heart makes before it even reaches your lips.

After several weeks of listening to the professor talk about every religion as if it was the ultimate truth, I was expecting to hear him give Christianity the same respect. But the atmosphere in the classroom shifted dramatically when we began studying the Christian faith. His remarks belittled the beliefs I held dear to my heart.

He not only dismissed the God of the Bible—but He also mocked Him. He spoke about Christians as if they were naïve and deceived. While there were other Believers in the class, less than a handful of us found the courage to speak up in defense of our faith.

That day, after another student commented about God answering prayers, the professor had launched his attack. His question about God having ears was meant to make us look foolish. In that moment, something rose up within me that couldn't stay silent.

After my response, the professor quickly moved on, but something profound had shifted within me. That moment of standing firm ignited a quiet confidence that continued to shape my faith for years to come. My passion for God deepened like roots finding water, and my understanding of His nature expanded beyond the confines of mere religion.

It was during a difficult period, years later, that I began to question whether my prayers were reaching God. Have you ever felt your words drifting upward like smoke, dissipating into an unresponsive sky? After repeatedly bringing Him the same request, I sat there in contemplation, whispering into the silence, wondering if God was listening to my desperate plea for help.

In reality, we all experience moments of uncertainty when God seems distant or His responses elusive. That's when doubt creeps in, casting dark shadows on our thinking. In the stillness of the night, we wrestle with thoughts, questioning His love or even His awareness of what we are going through.

It was during one of those times early one morning that I quietly whispered a prayer, "Are you listening to me Lord? Lord, are you hearing me?" The words fell from my lips like heavy raindrops, each one carrying the weight of my longing.

Suddenly, in my spirit, I heard God respond. *Yes, darling. My ears are attentive to your prayer.*

The word attentive means mindful, close, paying careful attention to something.

Wow. This truth—so simple yet profound—unfolded in my heart with newfound clarity. *He pays attention and is sensitive to my prayers.*

As I sat there pondering, I heard a few sighs coming from the side of my bed. My furry, white Maltese was in the background, his dark eyes peering at me with quiet expectation. Instead of his usual insistent bark, he watched me with patient hope, nudging my leg with his warm nose. Without giving it much thought, I headed towards his water dish. As I suspected, it was empty, so I quickly filled it up. He anxiously started drinking it until it was mostly gone. He was so thirsty.

It wasn't long after I walked over to my chair to pray and meditate that I felt my Maltese close, rubbing his fur against my feet. Sitting beside me while I prayed to start my day, he showed me how thankful he was.

At that moment, my mind went to the word attentive again. Then, I felt the Holy Spirit speak to me. A warmth spread through my chest as the truth settled in. *You are attentive to your dog's sighs and know his needs. How much more am I attentive to your needs?*

My soul felt at peace, as assurance washed over me. God doesn't just hear us—He listens with a Father's heart, recognizing even our unspoken needs. Though the answers to my prayers don't always come as quickly as I'd like, I know He is aware of where I am and what I need. He is not ignoring me and He is not forgetful.

I've come to treasure these silent conversations with God. The miracle isn't in getting immediate answers—it's in knowing He listens intently. He knows the subtle language of our souls— the sighs too deep for words, the questions we haven't fully formed, the doubts we're ashamed to voice—just as I sensed my dog's thirst without him having to bark loudly.

I've finally stopped straining to make God hear me. Instead, I sit in stillness, watching as my whispered worries, silent celebrations, and wordless wonderings become sacred

> He knows the subtle language of our souls—the sighs too deep for words, the questions we haven't fully formed, the doubts we're ashamed to voice

conversations with the One who catches every tear, translates every sigh, and treasures every word. God cherishes each whisper of my heart and cradles even my unspoken prayers in His heart. In this beautiful exchange of sighs and silence, I've discovered the most profound truth. *I am heard, I am known, and I am loved beyond measure.*

He hears you too, friend. Your silent fears. Your unspoken hopes. Your weary sighs. He hears them all and they all matter to Him.

> Your silent fears. Your unspoken hopes. Your weary sighs. He hears them all and they all matter to Him.

Lord,

Thank You for being the God who catches every whisper of my heart. Before a sigh escapes my lips, You've already understood its meaning. Before a tear forms, You've already collected it.

I stand in awe that You, Creator of the universe, lean in to hear my silent conversations—attentive to needs I haven't yet recognized in myself. Forgive me for questioning whether You were listening, for straining to make You hear what You've already understood completely.

Help me find peace in the space between prayers prayed and answers received. You always answer—sometimes differently than I expect, sometimes not in my timing, but always with my best in mind.

Let me trust Your heart when I can't see what You're doing. Let me rest in Your wisdom when Your ways seem unclear.

Thank You for hearing beyond my words, for seeing beyond my requests, and for loving beyond my understanding.

In the name of Jesus, Amen.

A Moment of Reflection

1. *Have there been experiences when you didn't feel seen or heard? How have they impacted your relationship with God?*

\
\
\
\

2. *What "sighs too deep for words" are you carrying today that you haven't fully expressed even in prayer? What would it mean to trust that God already understands these unspoken needs?*

\
\
\
\

3. *What prayer have you stopped praying because you believed it wasn't being heard? What might change if you viewed that silence not as absence but as God's attentive presence working in ways you can't yet see?*

\
\

____

____

4. *What subtle ways might God be communicating His presence and care in your life that you could be overlooking?*

____

____

____

5. *In what area of your life do you need to trust that God hears your heart's language even when your words fail you? What would it look like to rest in being heard rather than striving to be heard?*

____

____

____

6. *Consider a recent disappointment or unanswered prayer. How might God be attending to deeper needs beyond your specific request? What might He understand about your situation that you don't yet see?*

____

____

____

3

God Whispers

Sometimes the most profound moments of divine intervention come wrapped in the most ordinary packaging. A neighbor's unexpected offer to help just when you're overwhelmed, or a verse that pops into your mind in the middle of a sleepless night—can easily go unrecognized as the divine whispers they are. Yet it's in these gentle moments that we discover God's tender care for even our smallest concerns, reminding us that He is attentive to every detail of our lives.

> Sometimes the most profound moments of divine intervention come wrapped in the most ordinary packaging.

> *Then he was told, "Go, stand on the mountain at atten-*
> *tion before GOD. GOD will pass by."*
>
> *A hurricane wind ripped through the mountains and*
> *shattered the rocks before GOD, but GOD wasn't to be*
> *found in the wind; after the wind an earthquake, but*
> *GOD wasn't in the earthquake; and after the earth-*
> *quake fire, but GOD wasn't in the fire; and after the fire*
> *a gentle and quiet whisper.*
>
> I KINGS 19:11–12 (MSG)

Have you ever had a problem so small it seemed silly, yet so overwhelming it kept you awake at night? At nine years old, facing my first-ever camping trip as a Brownie Girl Scout, I discovered that if it mattered to me, it mattered to Him. No worry is too small for a love so great. What I was afraid would turn out as a moment of great embarrassment turned into my first encounter with the God Who sees.

Saturday morning arrived bright and invigorating. I bounced down the front steps, my small backpack bumping against me. Un-expectedly, I found myself climbing into the most luxurious vehicle I'd ever ridden in—a large, gleaming Cadillac sedan that belonged to one of my Girl Scout friends.

I couldn't contain my delight as we glided down the street, my fingers tracing the polished wood trim. The buttery leather seats seemed to swallow me whole, and every pothole felt like a gentle massage rather than a jarring bump. "This is how fancy people travel," I murmured, unable to hide my amazement. From behind the wheel came a warm laugh as my friend's mother caught my re-flection in the rearview mirror. My wonder-filled expression surely offered a reminder of how the ordinary can become someone else's extraordinary.

But the real adventure had actually begun the day before, in the familiar chaos of preparation. Our troop leaders had provided us with a detailed packing list that covered everything from toothbrushes to trail mix. Most items posed no problem—until I saw the words *sleeping bag*.

We owned exactly one sleeping bag, a forest-green monster that seemed to have a mind of its own. Every time I tried to roll it up and carry it, it rebelliously unraveled, slipping from my grasp and flopping open. We had nothing to tie it down with, so I wrestled with its unruly bulk, desperately trying to figure out how to carry it without it escaping again. My arms, thin as matchsticks, couldn't seem to wrangle the fluffy beast into submission.

"Come on, work with me here," I muttered, fighting the uncooperative bag for the fifth time. It slipped from my grasp again, unrolling with what I swear sounded like a chuckle.

The house had settled into its familiar nighttime quiet—the refrigerator's gentle hum, the tick of the clock, the distant sound of my parents' muffled conversation from their bedroom. But I laid there awake that evening, mentally running through my checklist one final time. *Flashlight? Check. Extra socks? Check. Toothbrush? Check. Sleeping bag?*

I clenched my jaw, a knot of dread tightening in my stomach as the scene played out in my mind like a slow-motion disaster. I'd arrive at the campground, my arms wrapped around this stubborn, bulky beast, battling its determined urge to unroll. The moment I lost my grip, it would seize the opportunity—sprawling open, knocking me off balance. My feet would forsake me, causing me to trip over the unruly bulk, sending me toppling forward in one graceless heap.

Laughter would ripple through the crowd, loud and impossible to ignore. I could see their faces, hear their mocking. Just the thought of it made my cheeks burn hot against my cool pillow, my pulse hammered in my ears. What a dreadful moment.

How am I going to carry that cumbersome sleeping bag without embarrassing myself by asking for help?

For an introverted girl like me, talking to an adult, let alone asking them for help, was daunting. Grownups seemed so intimidating.

Finally, after an endless amount of time mulling over this issue, in that space between worry and surrender, I did what children often do instinctively—I whispered a prayer into my pillow. "God, I really need help with this sleeping bag." A simple prayer, not eloquent or theologically sophisticated, just an honest plea from a little girl who hadn't been able to come up with a solution.

It wasn't long after, as I drifted into the twilight between wakefulness and sleep, a picture settled on my mind. It didn't flicker in and out like some passing thought. It lingered.

Settling into my mind with quiet certainty, as if waiting for me to truly see it.

I saw a leather belt. Sharp. Certain. As clear as if someone had placed it right in front of me.

My breath caught. Why hadn't I thought of that before?

I let out a long exhale, releasing the last of my worry into the stillness of the night. And with that, I drifted effortlessly into a sound sleep.

God had heard me. And He had answered.

The next morning, sunlight streamed through my curtains, warm and inviting, stirring me awake. I blinked against its brightness, the memory of last night's answer rushing back before my feet even touched the floor. Today was the day!

Without hesitation, I rushed to find my father and asked for one of his belts. Leather in hand, I wrapped it around the sleeping bag, fastening it tight. No struggle, no frustration—just a perfect, obedient roll.

I grinned. Victory tasted sweet. Not a worry in sight.

I was ready for adventure.

Since that moment, I've learned that no worry is too small for God. He listens. He answers. We just have to lean in, quiet our hearts, and tune in—like finding the right frequency on a radio. He is always speaking.

I've learned to listen for God's voice; His whispers are heard in the most unexpected places. He's spoken to me through dreams that linger like morning mist, their meaning unfolding gently, piece by piece, as the day awakens.

He whispers through the painted heavens—sunrises streaked with soft blush and gold, sunsets melting into violet and ember. In nature, during my photography walks, His voice emerges in the sound of a waterfall, the quiet rhythm of waves, the effortless beauty of a bird in flight.

Sometimes, He speaks through casual conversations that suddenly turn profound—a friend's comment, unlatching a door I hadn't even realized was closed. Other times, it's a movie scene that strikes me with unexpected wisdom. Or a billboard, bold and direct, as if placed there just for me, just for that moment.

Our Scripture from 1 Kings confirms what I've experienced firsthand—God's presence isn't just found in spectacular displays of power. It's not only in powerful winds strong enough to break rocks, not just in an earthquake's rumbling force, not strictly in a consuming fire's intensity. Instead, the Lord often chooses to speak in a gentle whisper, offering a quiet nudge that feels more like an invitation than a command, a soft impression that settles into our hearts when we're finally still enough to notice.

I think about young Samuel in the Old Testament (1 Samuel 3:4–5), lying in the temple, hearing a voice call his name in the darkness. Three times God called, and three times Samuel assumed it was his mentor Eli trying to get his attention. It wasn't until Eli's wisdom guided him that Samuel realized the Creator of the Universe was trying to have a conversation with him. How many divine whispers have slipped past our ears because we were expecting thunder?

God cares about every detail of our lives. The One who gave me answers for my nine-year-old camping worry so long ago, is the same one who sits with me in waiting rooms when test results are due or who whispers His peace when my thoughts race at 3:00 AM. My concerns matter to Him. Your concerns matter to Him. He's never too busy, never too distant to whisper exactly what we need to hear exactly when we need to hear it. We are never alone.

When my head is filled with stress or my heart cracks with grief, when I'm facing life's small battles or life-altering crossroads—He leans in closer, not away.

God never checks His watch. He never screens our calls. His presence is constant—His gentle reassurance quiets my racing thoughts: "You will never walk alone."

In our fast-paced, noise-saturated world, it's easy to miss sacred whispers. We're so accustomed to information shouting for our attention—phones buzzing, screens flashing, headlines screaming—that it's easy to miss the gentle sound of the voice that speaks peace into our chaos.

But what if we chose to tune in differently? What if we intentionally created quiet spaces in our days—not just for prayer or meditation, but for listening? What if we approached our daily experiences with expectant hearts, knowing that God delights in showing up in the ordinary moments of our lives?

That night before my camping trip, I fell asleep with a fresh solution provided by God. It may seem like a small thing now, but for that little girl, it was everything. It was my first real understanding that I am seen, known, and cared for by a God who pays attention to the details that matter to me.

As you go about your day, create small spaces of quiet. Put down your phone for a few minutes. Take a walk without earbuds. Notice what thoughts surface in the silence. Pay attention to the conversations that seem to address exactly what's on your heart. Watch for the "coincidences" that feel too perfectly timed to be random. They might be God whispers, sacred reminders that you are loved, guided, and never alone. Open your heart to receive them. In a loud world full of noise, sometimes the most important conversations happen in whispers. And sometimes, the most profound answers can come through something as simple as a leather belt wrapped around a sleeping bag—because that's how tenderly our God loves us. He pays attention to even the smallest details of our lives.

> In a loud world full of noise, sometimes the most important conversations happen in whispers.

God,

In the stillness of this moment, I come to You with an open heart. Thank you for being the God who sees—not just the polished parts of me that I present to the world, but every hidden corner, every quiet fear, every midnight worry.

When the noise of life threatens to drown out Your voice, teach me to create spaces of quiet. Help me recognize Your whispers in the ordinary moments of my days—in unexpected conversations, in the beauty of Your creation, in the gentle nudges that guide me home.

Thank you for caring about the details of my life. When I forget how much You love me, remind me of the times You've answered prayers I barely had words to form.

Lord, when my mind races with anxiety or my heart feels weighed down by grief, help me to draw near. Let me feel Your presence wrapping around me, Your gentle reassurance that I never walk alone.

Give me ears to hear You in the quiet moments, eyes to see Your hand at work in "coincidences," and let my heart be tuned to Your frequency.

May I carry the awareness of Your loving presence with me through each day, finding comfort in knowing that the God of the Universe cares about even the smallest details of my life.

In the name of Jesus, the One who taught us to listen, Amen.

A Moment of Reflection

1. *Has there been a time when you suddenly realized God had been attentive to details you thought were too small to matter?*

____

____

____

____

2. *What "noise" most often drowns out God's whispers in your daily life? What pulls your attention away?*

____

____

____

____

3. *Think of a recent worry that kept you awake at night. Have you brought it to God, or are you still trying to solve it on your own?*

____

____

____

____

4. *In what unexpected places or ordinary moments have you experienced God's presence the most? What made you able to notice Him there?*

____

____

____

____

5. *When you think about hearing God's voice, what do you feel—comfort, doubt, longing, fear? Where does that feeling come from?*

____

____

____

____

6. *Take a quiet moment right now and ask God what He wants to say about your current situation. What comes to mind?*

____

____

____

____

4

Divine Interruptions

Have you ever noticed how the most profound moments in life often arrive unannounced? That unexpected detour leading to a life-changing encounter, the phone call that shifts your entire day, or the stranger's need that somehow becomes your divine assignment? These interruptions aren't accidents but God's masterful orchestration weaving His purposes into the fabric of our busy lives.

> *When she heard about Jesus, she came up behind him in the crowd and touched his cloak, because she thought, "If I just touch his clothes, I will be healed." Immediately her bleeding stopped and she felt in her body that she was freed from her suffering.*
>
> *At once Jesus realized that power had gone out from him. He turned around in the crowd and asked, "Who touched my clothes?"*
>
> *"You see the people crowding against you," his disciples answered, "and yet you can ask, 'Who touched me?'"*

But Jesus kept looking around to see who had done it.

Then the woman, knowing what had happened to her, came and fell at his feet and, trembling with fear, told him the whole truth. He said to her, "Daughter, your faith has healed you. Go in peace and be freed from your suffering"

MARK 5:27–34 (NIV)

The urgent call of, "Mom!" It never fails. The moment I get on the phone, an emergency happens or the kids require my undivided attention.

Interruptions. The very word sends a ripple of tension across our shoulders. I have never met anyone who welcomes them with open arms. Instead, they're typically greeted with heavy sighs and furrowed brows.

Who hasn't experienced a child having a nightmare just as you've fallen into deep sleep? A neighbor knocking on your door just as you've settled in with your morning coffee? The jarring ring of a phone during a moment of prayer or reflection?

By their very nature, interruptions are inconvenient intrusions, disrupting our focus and hindering progress. They often leave us stranded between intention and completion, usually accompanied by frustration and annoyance.

As a young mother, I discovered children have an uncanny knack for interruption. Like tiny experts equipped with invisible sensors, they've perfected the timing game, choosing to emerge with needs just when we're laser-focused on something crucial. It's at those moments that they unintentionally, yet skillfully, have a need for something urgent.

This became my daily reality when my kids were little. It was always something. Whether it was a shoe that needed to be tied, starvation requiring an immediate snack, or a philosophical question about why the sky isn't green—it just couldn't wait. Their tugging tiny hands and persistent little voices became impossible to ignore as my carefully constructed mental to-do list dissolved like sugar in hot tea. Plans became more like gentle suggestions when little ones were involved, but I was learning to pause and see what was really important in those moments—learning this was just a season that wouldn't last forever.

Years later, I'd discover that interruptions never really stop coming; they just change form. Disruptions, I've learned, are as inevitable as changing seasons—unexpected circumstances that halt us in our tracks, sometimes redirecting our attention in better directions than we'd planned.

The gospels paint a vivid portrait of Jesus living a life woven with "interruptions." In Mark 5, we witness Jesus surrounded by a sea of expectant faces, the air thick with hope and desperation, when Jairus, a synagogue leader, cut through the crowd. With eyes hollow from sleepless nights at his daughter's bedside, he falls before Jesus, his status stripped away by desperation. He pleads with Jesus to leave the multitude and come pray for his dying daughter.

As Jesus threads His way through the pressing multitude, following Jairus toward what seems the day's divine appointment, another "interruption" emerges. Through the clamor of voices and bodies pressing in, Jesus stops suddenly, something unseen catching His attention. "Who touched Me?" He asks, His voice carrying over the confused murmurs of the crowd.

Peter, practical and somewhat shocked by his question, gestures to the masses surrounding them. "Master, the people are crowding and pressing against you." His unspoken question hangs in the air. *How could anyone not be touching you?*

But Jesus persists. "Someone touched me; I know that power has gone out of me." His words reveal a profound distinction—this wasn't the casual brush of the jostling crowd but a touch infused with desperate faith.

Isn't it remarkable that amid the suffocating press of needy humanity, Jesus discerns the gentle, trembling touch of one fragile woman? A woman drained of strength, health, and hope by twelve long years of unstoppable bleeding? It was the tug from an unclean woman on the hem of His garment that drew Christ's attention.

With eyes that saw beyond her illness to her worth, Jesus pauses the urgent journey to Jairus' home. He creates a holy pause in time, a sacred space where this suffering woman is truly seen, perhaps for the first time in twelve painful years. To Jesus, she is not unclean. To Jesus, she is not a sinner or lawbreaker. To Jesus, she is not an interruption—she is the appointment.

In those days, a woman with bleeding was marked as unclean, forbidden from entering the temple's courts, forced to withdraw from community into a prison of isolation. For twelve years—*imagine the weight of four thousand lonely days*—this woman had lived as an outcast. According to these same laws, her touch should have rendered Jesus ritually impure.

This woman had weathered not just the storm of physical suffering and drained resources, but the drought of human connection. Can you feel the ache of her loneliness? The yearning for a single touch that didn't pull away? How divinely orchestrated that this encounter unfolds before Jairus, the very synagogue leader who enforced her isolation. Perhaps Jesus was offering a living parable in compassion, challenging the leader's strict religious rules while his own heart was softened by personal crisis.

With words that wash away twelve years of shame, Jesus calls this woman out of hiding, meets her trembling gaze, and speaks a single word: "Daughter." This moment—the only time in all

Scripture where Jesus addresses a woman as "daughter"—becomes her redemption song. In an instant, she's no longer an outcast—she's family. After years of being pushed to the margins, He welcomes her back into belonging, restoring her place in the human family with the gentleness of a father's love.

Jesus then affirms the courage behind her actions, celebrating the bold steps she took despite her weakness to reach out in faith. This woman's miracle wasn't simply bestowed as an act of divine compassion. Rather, it came when her desperate faith met bold action, bringing the healing she had sought for so long.

- She pressed through physical weakness and social barriers, her determination stronger than her depleted body.

- She chose to enter a crowd that had labeled her untouchable, risking further rejection.

- She defied her assigned place of isolation, stepping beyond its boundaries.

- Finally, surrounded by potential judgment and a religious authority who could condemn her, she confessed her actions openly. Vulnerability became her final act of courage.

This woman wasn't just grabbing at Jesus's clothing randomly. Her fingers sought the tzitzit—the sacred fringes on his Jewish tallit that symbolized God's promises and power. These knotted threads represented all 613 commandments, including God's promises of healing.[1] When she touched them, she was literally desperately reaching for her promise.

---

1 "The Tallit: Spiritual Significance," My Jewish Learning, September 14, 2017, https://www.myjewishlearning.com/article/the-tallit-spiritual-significance/.

Jesus encountered interruptions constantly, yet moved through them with the grace of one who recognized divine orchestration in human chaos. Followed endlessly by people whose needs screamed for attention, Jesus perceived God's fingerprints in these "interruptions," seeing them not as burdens that depleted but as appointments that fulfilled His purpose.

We often confine our understanding of ministry to formal roles—preaching from pulpits, teaching Sunday school classes, or facilitating small groups. But have we constructed too small a box for God's work through us? How many holy moments have slipped through our fingers because we labeled them disruptions to our schedule or because weariness made us blind to the divine appointment disguised as inconvenience?

When I look back at the most meaningful encounters in my life, so many began as inconvenient interruptions. An unexpected call that resulted in divine impartation of much-needed wisdom. A sudden stop to my day because someone was in desperate need of prayer—moments that could be looked at as interruptions become channels of God's love and grace.

> How many holy moments have slipped through our fingers because we labeled them disruptions to our schedule or because weariness made us blind to the divine appointment disguised as inconvenience?

How often have I myself interrupted someone's schedule and been the recipient of much-needed support? The stranger who paused their errands to help when my car broke down. The friend who answered my late-night call despite having an early morning commitment. These holy interruptions weave through our lives, revealing glimpses of God's intricate design.

> When we surrender our carefully guarded time to Him, even our disruptions become opportunities for His power to flow.

Spirit-led living places God in control of our moments, our schedules, and our interruptions. When we surrender our carefully guarded time to Him, even our disruptions become opportunities for His power to flow. Perhaps today's interruption is actually tomorrow's testimony waiting to unfold.

Father,

Open my eyes to see Your divine purpose in each interruption that comes my way. When my plans are disrupted and my schedule derailed, whisper to my heart that these moments may be the very appointments You've orchestrated. Soften my impatience and transform my frustration into expectancy.

Holy Spirit, gently remind me that when I surrendered my life to You, I invited You to direct my steps—even when they lead me down unexpected paths. Give me wisdom to discern the holy opportunities that may be hidden in interruptions, and the courage to step into them with love and grace. May I become so attuned to Your voice that I recognize those divine moments when You're asking me to be Your hands, Your voice, Your heart to someone in need. Lord, help me to remember that sometimes the greatest ministry happens not in my carefully planned moments, but in the beautiful interruptions You send my way.

In Jesus' Name. Amen.

A Moment of Reflection

1. In what areas of your life do you tend to resist interruptions?
    Does that reveal anything about your expectations or pace?

    ____

    ____

    ____

    ____

2. What "hem of His garment" are you reaching for today? What
    promise from God's Word are you clinging to in faith?

    ____

    ____

    ____

    ____

3. What interruption in your life felt like a setback, but turned out
    to be a divine interruption?

    ____

    ____

    ____

    ____

4. *When have you felt overlooked or dismissed in a moment of need?
    How might that experience help you recognize someone else's
    silent reach for hope?*

____

____

____

____

5. *The woman with the issue of blood took several courageous steps of
    faith. Which of her steps challenge you most in your own spiritual
    journey?*

____

____

____

____

6. *In what ways might God be using your interruptions of others to
    bring His presence into their lives?*

____

____

____

____

5

Interruptions or Invitations?

The phone rings just as you're sitting down for dinner after an exhausting day. Your child needs help with homework while deadlines loom. Or you were finally sitting down after a long day only to hear those words, "Could you do me a favor?"

We've all felt that familiar tension—the silent battle between our carefully guarded time and someone else's need. In that split second between request and response lives a sacred opportunity that too often goes unrecognized. The tension between our carefully planned lives and these interruptions reveals something deeper in our hearts.

> *"'For I was hungry and you gave me something to eat, I was thirsty and you gave me something to drink, I was a stranger and you invited me in, I needed clothes and you clothed me, I was sick and you looked after me, I was in prison and you came to visit me.'*
>
> *"Then the righteous will answer him, 'Lord, when did we see you hungry and feed you, or thirsty and give you*

> *something to drink? When did we see you a stranger and invite you in, or needing clothes and clothe you? When did we see you sick or in prison and go to visit you?'*
>
> *"The King will reply, 'Truly I tell you, whatever you did for one of the least of these brothers and sisters of mine, you did for me.'"*
>
> MATTHEW 25:35–40 (NIV)

"Could you help me?" The words came through my phone, her voice small and hesitant. I could hear the discomfort in my friend's tone, the subtle pause before asking. For a split second, I stared at my phone, my heart sinking just a little. My planner sat open beside me, every hour already spoken for. I'd mapped out the day with precision—emails, errands, writing blocks—all lined up like dominoes. One favor, even a small one, would tip the whole thing.

I wasn't upset by the request itself. Not at all. I was simply caught off guard by how tightly I'd packed my day, leaving little room for the unexpected. And while I felt the tension of that shift, what stirred most deeply in me wasn't frustration with my friend, but a quiet conviction: I want to live with enough margin to say yes when it matters. It was that familiar tug—the ache of wanting to be available, yet realizing I'd left myself no room. Silently, I sighed under my breath, knowing her need mattered more than the carefully mapped goals I'd laid out for the day.

Like seasons of growth, requests for help often arrive when we feel least equipped—when our energy is low, our schedules full, and our patience thin. In that weighted pause between request and response, while my friend waited silently on the other end, I sensed an invitation—not just to rearrange my day, but to realign my heart.

Interruptions, I've come to realize, are often sacred. They till the soil of our tightly held plans and plant seeds of compassion, flexibility, and grace. These moments don't always bear fruit immediately, but over time, they soften our rigidity and cultivate a heart more attuned to God's love.

My mother understood this instinctively. A woman with the gift of serving, she instilled in me an understanding of true giving. Although service isn't my inherent gift, I learned by watching her exemplify selfless serving, never expecting anything in return. For her, a favor was never done because it was convenient, the timing was right, or because she had the energy. She helped others simply when asked and chose to respond with an open heart.

In fact, one day she said to me, "Favors, by their very nature, are always inconvenient." She taught me that our compassion and commitment to others are best demonstrated during their times of need, even when it's difficult for us to help them.

> "Favors, by their very nature, are always inconvenient." She taught me that our compassion and commitment to others are best demonstrated during their times of need, even when it's difficult for us to help them.

She was a hardworking woman, always on the go. She was the type of person who enjoyed being with people and demonstrated her love through countless acts of service. Whether welcoming immigrants into our home until they were settled, delivering home-cooked meals to someone sick, or providing transportation after her exhausting workday, I never once heard her decline a request for help. Even more remarkable, she never mentioned her kindness toward those who later spoke poorly of her, nor did I ever hear her complain about feeling used.

Despite decades in a church, her name never graced a leadership roster or committee list. While others collected titles, her seeds of service grew silently in the soil of everyday life. The fruit of her labor remains hidden in God's heart and in the lives she touched—remembered only by the Creator who saw each act and those who received her quiet ministry. Serving wasn't tied to programs or confined within institutional walls; it flowed naturally from who she was, often going unnoticed by all but those whose lives she changed.

One story my daughter often shares captures this woman's essence perfectly. While visiting the small town where she was born, they were warmly greeted by a woman with tears in her eyes. She recounted how my mother had been her lifeline during a tough time, so much so that she credited her for being alive. My mother's unwavering dedication to helping others left a legacy that touched many.

We often place ministry in a box. We think of it solely as the work we deliberately choose to do within the walls of a church building or a nonprofit institution, such as serving at a food bank. But Jesus did ministry differently. To Jesus, ministry was a lifestyle where he met the needs of people in a relational context. Christ's ministry often happened spontaneously, as people found Him after He had escaped to find rest after a full day of giving.

Requests happened at the most inopportune times, often when He was on his way somewhere with a mission in mind. One example of this was when He was on His way to Jairus' house to heal the religious leader's daughter, who was dying. The fact is, Jesus was never too busy to pause and minister to the needs of those who ended up on His path.

Interruption after interruption, Jesus did not allow an agenda to dictate His journey. Neither did He allow the needs of the people to determine His next step. Instead, Jesus lived a life led by the Holy Spirit, never hesitating to pause and listen to the cries of people around Him. Attuned to the Father, Jesus discerned every need along the way and recognized who needed His attention. Ultimately, Christ's life mission was about serving. In Mark 10:45 we're told, *"Jesus said, 'The Son of Man did not come to be served, but to serve.'"*

Serving others is a privilege set before us daily. Ministry happens at kitchen tables, in grocery store aisles, and through phone calls that interrupt our day. Each interruption invites us to see beyond our schedules to God's greater purpose. When the phone rings at an inconvenient hour or a neighbor knocks unexpectedly, we may be standing at a sacred crossroads—not facing a disruption, but a divine appointment carefully arranged by the One who sees both our plans and the hidden needs around us. In these moments of pause, we have the chance to make a difference we may never see—that one day may impact souls we'll never meet. The question isn't whether we have time to serve, but whether we'll recognize the eternal opportunity hidden within the momentary inconvenience.

> When the phone rings at an inconvenient hour or a neighbor knocks unexpectedly, we may be standing at a sacred crossroads— not facing a disruption, but a divine appointment carefully arranged by the One who sees both our plans and the hidden needs around us.

Father,

Forgive me for the times I've sighed when my phone rang unexpectedly or when someone approached with need in their eyes. How often have I missed Your face in theirs? How many divine appointments have I dismissed as mere interruptions?

Lord, when I feel that tension between my carefully guarded schedule and someone else's need, slow my racing thoughts. Help me remember that in that weighted pause between request and response lies an opportunity to plant a sacred seed. Let me see beyond my color-coded calendar to the eternal purpose You're weaving through these moments.

Jesus, You never saw people as interruptions. Even when exhausted, even when heading somewhere important, You paused for the unseen, the overlooked, the desperate. Give me Your eyes to recognize these holy invitations hidden within everyday requests. When I'm tempted to protect my time and energy, remind me that Your strength flows most powerfully through my willingness to be inconvenienced.

Holy Spirit, cultivate in me a servant's heart—that beautiful willingness to help without recognition, to serve without complaint, to give without expectation of return. Increase my compassion, transform any rigidity I have into flexibility, and turn my carefully fenced life into open ground where Your love flows freely.

May I remember that true ministry rarely happens according to plan. It happens in unexpected ways, in unexpected circumstances, in the quiet offerings of help that no committee will ever recognize.

Lord, help me recognize opportunities to serve You by serving others. Instead of seeing these sudden requests as inconvenient, help me see them as divine appointments to sow into Your Kingdom. The question isn't whether I have time—it's whether I'll recognize You in the moment when You knock at my door disguised as interruption.

In the name of Jesus, who came not to be served, but to serve. Amen.

A Moment of Reflection

1. *In what ways have you separated "ministry" from everyday life? Have you missed opportunities to serve because they didn't fit your definition of ministry?*

____

____

____

____

2. *Can you think of a time when someone's interruption felt intrusive. What might God have been trying to accomplish through their need? How would seeing it as a divine appointment have changed your response?*

____

____

____

____

3. *What single change to your daily routine could create space to respond to unexpected needs with grace instead of frustration?*

____

____

4. *How has your relationship with time shaped your willingness to serve? What shift in perspective would help you make margin for divine interruptions?*

5. *What area of control do you most resist surrendering when interrupted—your time, energy, comfort, or something deeper?*

6. *When has someone's unexpected act of service deeply impacted you? Have you ever told them what it meant?*

SECTION II

EXPERIENCING GOD'S LOVE is about discovering His heart—revealed in the whisper of His presence and in the hands of His people. When the blinders fall, you see the truth: He was never far away. He's been here all along, relentless in His love for you. That love shows up—in kindness that reaches, compassion that listens, grace that meets you exactly where you are. Every gesture, every moment becomes an echo of the One who will not let you go.

6

Ask Me for the Moon

In the sacred space between our whispered desires and God's boundless provision lies an invitation that changes everything. What if your boldest prayers aren't too extravagant for God, but rather too confined by your own hesitation?

> **"Ask for a sign from your GOD. Ask anything. Be extravagant. Ask for the moon!"**
>
> ISAIAH 7:11 (MSG)

On the morning of July 11, 2016, I awoke from a deep sleep to the sound of my phone ringing. It was my daughter, Tiffany. She was in labor. After 9 months of waiting the day had finally come. Her firstborn was on the way.

I jumped out of bed, my heart racing with excitement. My head was spinning as I reached for the bag I had packed and repacked a dozen times. My fingers fumbled through it, pulling out each item as my eyes darted nervously, scrutinizing the choices I had made on what to take.

Suddenly I was second-guessing myself. Inside were all the things I thought I'd need for the long hours ahead—phone chargers, a jacket, colorful lollipops, crunchy snacks to calm my nerves. But did I pack enough snacks? What if I forgot something important?

I stopped myself, took a deep breath, and whispered a quick prayer. The spinning stopped. My breathing slowed, and the chaos in my mind quieted. Within minutes, my husband Jim, my oldest daughter Jessica, and I were out the door and on our way to the hospital.

Walking into the hospital, we asked the Lord for a Scripture for the day. We specifically looked for passages with chapter 7 and verse 11, representing our grandchild's soon-to-be birthdate. After reading several possibilities, Jessica read Isaiah 7:11 from the Message Bible. The Scripture seemed to leap out at us. It felt like we received a rhema word—a word brought to life by the Holy Spirit to guide us in our specific situation. The Greek word rhema (ῥῆμα) means "utterance" or "spoken word." It's a term referring to the spoken word of God, or a specific word from the Holy Spirit.

I love it when words are highlighted and magnified, seeming to jump off the page! On that day, the message I read "landed in my spirit."

GOD spoke again to Ahaz. This time he said, "Ask for a sign from your GOD. Ask anything. Be extravagant. Ask for the moon!"

ISAIAH 7:10–11 (MSG)

It was a Scripture I had never really noticed before and reading it in the Message translation was a real eye-opener for me. I was not using this Scripture as a formula. Rather, I saw it as a response to

"Ask for a sign from your GOD. Ask anything. Be extravagant."

an invitation to converse with God about our needs and our desires. Moreover, as a loving Father, His longing to fulfill our desires became unmistakenly clear in that moment. It also became evident to me that His desire was for us not to hold back when we made our requests known to him, but rather to be extravagant in our asking.

I found myself pondering those words and thinking about other Scriptures where God encourages us to ask Him for what we want. Scriptures such as 1 John 5:14 and others came to mind.

And how bold and free we then become in his presence, freely asking according to his will, sure that he's listening. And if we're confident that he's listening, we know that what we've asked for is as good as ours.

1 JOHN 5:14–15 (MSG)

The more I read, the more it felt like God was saying, "Don't be shy! Don't limit yourself by asking just for what you need. I own it all and I enjoy giving you the things you ask for." What a loving God He is!

As we made our way to the hospital room, I was overwhelmed with a fresh revelation of how much God delights in our happiness. Like a good father, He takes pleasure in responding to our needs and desires.

Stepping into the birthing suite, a tangible excitement filled the air. The baby unit stood ready, softly lit, and lined with instruments ready to monitor our new granddaughter's first moments of life—her breaths and heartbeats. The scene made it plain: she was almost here.

Initially, everything was going smoothly. However, it didn't take long to notice that the contractions, while frequent, weren't yielding the progress we hoped for. The hands on the clock inched forward while my daughter's pain became more intense. In the dimness of the room, tension coiled around us, and unspoken prayers continuously reached towards heaven. My mother's heart ached, wishing I could absorb her pain and bring her relief. I wanted it to end soon with the baby's safe and healthy arrival.

Although she was determined, braving natural childbirth was tougher than my daughter had anticipated, especially with the lack of progress. The weariness on her face made it clear that her high tolerance for pain was reaching its limits. Finally, at her doctor's suggestion, Tiffany and her husband Nick decided it was time to consider an alternative plan.

Until that moment, we had fervently prayed and recited Scripture over the birth, weaving our faith into the long hours that ticked by. It felt like our prayers and declarations of His Word weren't working. Despite our heartfelt efforts, progress remained minimal and it was time for us to leave the room as they prepared to move forward with the procedure. Our footsteps dragged, hints of disappointment and weariness chipping away at our initial excitement as we headed to the little café downstairs.

Deciding what to eat felt monumental as my heart and thoughts remained with Tiffany, imagining what she was going through. Despite the hours since my last meal, I wasn't even sure if I felt hungry. The weight of emotions and concern overshadowed my physical needs.

As I lingered in the café, each moment seemed to heighten my restlessness, gradually fragmenting the peace I was trying to hold onto. Turning to Jim, I expressed my unease saying, "The only thing I want to do is get back up there to be with them." Within a few moments he was leading us back to the birthing room.

Walking down the hallway, chatting about different things, my mind began to wander. Suddenly, a surge of determination welled up within me, and a prayer burst forth from my lips. "Father, you gave us Isaiah 7:11 for today and it says, 'Ask Me anything.' You said in Your word 'be extravagant' so I am asking You for the progression of this birth to occur without any further procedure or any other complications!"

It wasn't a demand. Rather, it was a moment of realigning my soul with the word God had given me for that day. At that moment, I shifted from a place of concern and creeping fear to one of confidence, positioning myself to stand in faith as His daughter, despite what I was seeing. My eyes locked with unwavering determination; a fierce resolve ignited my heart. The words we had received became my anchor once again, steadfast and unyielding, even when the circumstances seemed to veer off course.

As we stepped back into the waiting room, we were anxiously greeted with good news. Remarkably, during the 20 minutes we were away, my daughter had transitioned into the final stage of labor and was

> At that moment, I shifted from a place of concern and creeping fear to one of confidence, positioning myself to stand in faith as His daughter, despite what I was seeing. My eyes locked with unwavering determination; a fierce resolve ignited my heart.

ready for delivery. An hour later, our hearts swelled with emotion as we stood in awe, witnessing our newborn grandbaby's first breaths. Her delicate hands and feet stretched as she vocalized her protest against leaving the warm cocoon she had known for nine months. Jewel's first cry was like a melody, her presence filling the room with overwhelming joy. It was one of the most precious and unforgettable moments of our lives, a celebration of new beginnings and a true testament to standing in faith when circumstances take unexpected turns.

Standing there quietly, immersed in this life-changing event, I felt God's warm, gentle Presence enveloping us. It was as if He were softly whispering, "I treasure being part of every facet of your life. Hearing you share the desires of your heart moves My heart. And fulfilling your desires gives me pleasure."

As a loving Father, He delights in hearing us ask, not only for what we need, but also for what we want. God's longing is to journey with us through every situation, encouraging us to seek Him and ask for insight into His perfect will. In moments of doubt, as we delve into His Word, His promises unfold like a comforting embrace, re-assuring us that we are never truly alone. God stands at the threshold of possibility, urging us beyond our timid, measured prayers into valiant requests that reflect His limitless nature—a God who delights in giving immeasurably more.

Loving Father,

My heart stills in wonder at Your invitation to ask boldly—not with hesitation, but with the confident expectation of a beloved child. How often I have approached You with carefully measured requests, afraid to voice the deepest desires You Yourself have planted within me.

Today, I dare to lift my eyes beyond what seems reasonable or possible. Like a child gazing at the moon in wonder, I open my hands to receive what only You can give. When circumstances suggest retreat and fear whispers that I've asked too much, anchor me in the truth of Your Word that beckons me to "be extravagant" in my requests, believing that You want me to believe You for the impossible because You are the God of the impossible.

In those sacred moments when situations seem too difficult and progress too slow, when I'm tempted to settle for less than Your best, remind me that You delight in my boldest prayers. Teach me to realign my soul with the promises You've spoken over my life, shifting from a place of worry and doubt to one of unwavering confidence in Your character.

Thank You for being present in every facet of my journey—not just as an observer, but as an active participant who treasures being invited into my deepest longings. When I stand in awe of unexpected blessings, let me remember that Your desire to fulfill the wishes of my heart exceeds even my desire to see them granted.

In Your presence, I find courage to voice what I scarcely dare to hope for, knowing You are an extravagant giver who never withholds good from Your children. Thank You for being such a good Father, whose joy is found in giving far beyond what I could ask or imagine. Amen.

A Moment of Reflection

1. *What desire has God placed in your heart that seems too extravagant to voice aloud? What would happen if you dared to "ask for the moon" regarding this longing?*

---

2. *What Scripture might God be highlighting for your current circumstances? Can you stand firmly on its promise regardless of what you see?*

---

3. *In what areas of your life have you been praying "safe" prayers—requests carefully measured to avoid disappointment?*

---

4. *This chapter describes a moment of shifting "from a place of concern and creeping fear to one of confidence." Where do you need this kind of spiritual realignment today?*

____

____

____

____

5. *God's invitation to "ask for the moon" reveals His character as an abundantly generous Father. How has God's extravagant provision surprised you in the past?*

____

____

____

____

6. *What impossible situation are you facing that needs an "Isaiah 7:11 prayer"—a bold request that aligns with God's character and promises?*

____

____

____

____

7

The Sound of Grace

I'd spent a lifetime being my own harshest critic, convinced that perfectionism was the only acceptable standard. Then one night, God interrupted my sleep with words that taught me—the sound of grace.

> *But You, O Lord, are a God [who protects and is] merciful and gracious, Slow to anger and abounding in lovingkindness and truth.*
>
> PSALM 86:15 (AMP)

"It's okay you lost your notebook."

The words from the dream echoed, resonating in my soul, as if someone were imprinting them into the creases of a lost memory. In my dream, these words were spoken to me by an adult while I was a child—not with the sharp reprimand I was accustomed to, but with a gentleness unfamiliar to me.

I woke up with a jolt. My body tensed instinctively, painful feelings flooding my heart at the mere thought of consequences from losing an important object. I trembled in the darkness, my mind racing to catalog what I'd done wrong.

Then, amid the emotional turmoil, my focus shifted to the unfamiliar voice's gentle, reassuring tone. This voice, so different from what I was used to hearing when I made a mistake, enveloped me in an unexpected comfort. I realized that losing a notebook wasn't catastrophic. No one seethed with anger. Instead, the gentle voice conveyed that the situation could be easily mended.

This revelation not only astounded me, but flooded me with love. I wept uncontrollably at the tenderness in the voice—so foreign to anything I'd ever heard before. His calm and non-condescending tone were reassuring and healing.

Right then, something became clear. This is how mistakes should have been addressed—with gentleness rather than criticism, with patience instead of frustration, and with the quiet assurance that we'd figure it out together rather than the isolating feeling that I had failed.

My distress transported me back to childhood moments—times when getting distracted or moving too slowly resulted in reprimand. Memories flashed of overwhelming fear and the practiced art of hiding emotions. I'd learned early not to burden others, already carrying their own heavy loads of pain.

Even though my parents worked hard to meet all my physical needs, the pressures and stressors of life blinded them to the emotional struggles others were experiencing. My deep emotions arising from the crisis and trauma around me went unnoticed as the adults in my life wrestled with their own. How could they recognize in me, what they couldn't see in themselves? Their own emotions lay buried beneath resilient exteriors, suppressed by years of practiced survival.

When adults are overwhelmed by their own pain, they may unintentionally lean on their children to shoulder responsibilities never meant for them. This dynamic often results in children growing into adults who reflexively take on others' burdens as their own. Consequently, these children develop heightened anxiety both in childhood and adulthood, making it nearly impossible to manage their own emotions—much less attend to the emotional needs of those who depend on them. The cycle continues until someone recognizes and breaks this pattern.

The morning of my dream, I pondered. *What was God saying to me?* I had heard the words so clearly: *It's okay that you lost your notebook.* Then, like lightning illuminating a darkened landscape, understanding struck. The pieces began to fit as I heard, a simple question forming in my consciousness. *How many times do you lose things?*

The question deeply pierced my core identity. Shame washed over me, followed by self-directed anger at my perpetual habit of misplacing phones, keys—mine and my husband's—and the ritual of returning to the house, sometimes twice, for forgotten items. Though not accusatory, the question exposed a raw nerve.

As pieces of my past became clear, I realized how children respond to early wounds in seemingly opposite ways—some through visible disorganization, others through rigid perfectionism. I could see my own story reflected in these patterns throughout different seasons of my life, pieces of a puzzle finally forming a coherent picture.

It's okay that you lost your notebook.

These words illuminated where my heart needed healing from the crushing weight of perfectionism. A place where I felt the gentle touch of God's love, bringing me to an awareness of why I expected so much from myself. The shame was not coming from God. It wasn't a shaming gesture, but a tender

> **The shame was not coming from God.**

one—stirring deep emotional memories buried in my heart, needing to come to the forefront.

The Holy Spirit was lovingly pointing out my discrepancies, imperfections, and failures—not to condemn me but to reveal how I demanded more of myself than He ever did. I needed to accept my humanity! Where I was haunted by my shortcomings, expecting perfection from myself, He offered a perspective that was very different from mine. While I focused on failure, He offered grace. Where I condemned my mistakes, He cherished my love for learning.

It's okay that you lost your notebook.

I found myself exhaling deeply, granting myself the right to be human—the right to fail, to lose my keys, to make mistakes. For years, unrealistic expectations had kept me bound to anxiety, but now I could release them one by one. This permission to be human was a practice I needed to implement daily. God accepted me as I am; I needed to accept myself without shame for my weaknesses.

> I found myself exhaling deeply, granting myself the right to be human— the right to fail, to lose my keys, to make mistakes.

No more self-judgement and condemnation. These only drained my energy and became stumbling blocks, obscuring my view of the strengths and competence God had given me. They were in essence, self-sabotage. Instead, I made a choice to extend myself the same grace God so freely extended me—drinking deeply from His limitless fountain of acceptance. The loving grace He never stops extending to you and me.

Dearest Father,

I feel Your gentle presence reminding me that You created me human, not flawless. Thank You for never sighing in exasperation when I make the same mistakes again and again. While I grow impatient with my own imperfections, You remain steadfast—slow to anger, abounding in compassion.

How liberating it is to realize that the perfection I've been chasing was never something You required of me. The standards that have kept me anxious and afraid, rehearsing failures and fearing mistakes—these were never Your expectations, but chains I fashioned for myself. In Your eyes, my stumbling is not catastrophic but simply learning to walk in grace.

Today, I choose to extend to myself the same tender acceptance You have always offered me. Loosen the grip of these unreasonable expectations that have wound themselves around my heart. Replace the voices of condemnation with Your whisper, "It's okay." Free me to live in the spacious freedom of being fully human, fully loved, and fully welcomed—not despite my imperfections, but with them held gently in Your loving hands.

In Jesus' Name. Amen.

A Moment of Reflection

1. *Do you struggle with shame after making a mistake?*

    ____

    ____

    ____

    ____

2. *Consider the voices that shaped your childhood understanding of mistakes. How do those voices differ from God's voice described in Psalm 86:15?*

    ____

    ____

    ____

    ____

3. *What "lost notebooks" in your life—small mistakes or failures— continue to haunt you? How would it feel to hear God say, "It's okay" about each one?*

    ____

    ____

    ____

    ____

4. *In what areas of your life do you hold yourself to standards of perfection that God doesn't require of you?*

____

____

____

____

5. *How might your relationships transform if you approached mistakes—both yours and others'—with God's gentleness?*

____

____

____

____

6. *How could you begin to speak to yourself—and respond to your mistakes—with the same grace God extends to you?*

____

____

____

____

8

Unraveled By Love

Silence. In a house full of children, it's the most suspicious sound. It's in these ordinary moments of family life, where discipline dissolves into laughter and shame transforms into grace, that I've glimpsed profound truths about God's patient love. Just when we think we've got it all figured out, life throws us a four-year-old with a pillow stuffed down her pants to remind us of what's really important—love, laughter, life.

> *May He grant you out of the riches of His glory, to be strengthened and spiritually energized with power through His Spirit in your inner self, [indwelling your innermost being and personality], so that Christ may dwell in your hearts through your faith. And may you, having been [deeply] rooted and [securely] grounded in love, be fully capable of comprehending with all the saints (God's people) the width and length and height and depth of His love [fully experiencing that amazing, endless love].*
>
> EPHESIANS 3:16–18 (AMP)

Crayons scattered across the floor. The unmistakable silence that signals trouble brewing, somewhere. A trail of half-eaten snacks. Could raising three daughters really be this chaotic? My choice to homeschool all three girls turned out nothing like I'd imagined when I enthusiastically decided to do so. *What was I thinking?*

Between lesson plans and Band-aids®, math problems and heart-to-heart talks, those unpredictable days taught me more about love than any parenting book ever could. Raising my three spirited girls meant surrendering to the beautiful pandemonium of the unexpected—no two days ever played by the same rules.

But even before our homeschooling adventure, I treasured my time with them so much that I occasionally declared "mother–daughter days"—school absences justified by nothing more than the need for connection.

At one point, we met our family deductible in the first month of the year due to a broken arm, a sprained ankle, and a sprained finger. Our pediatrician came to know each daughter's personality, greeting us with a warm, "Which of my favorite patients do I get to see today?"

The younger two, only two years apart, were inseparable. In our house, silence was not golden. Silence was my cue that the girls were up to something. When they put their heads together, trouble was never far away. Their boundless imaginations and creativity sparked limitless, and sometimes disruptive exploits.

One afternoon, after a quiet spell that stretched suspiciously long, I went looking for the younger two, only to find them huddled together, whispers dissolving into guilty giggles. In the days before long explanations replaced spanking, I walked away with a warning that they were about to be paddled, my voice carrying that unmistakable mom-means-business tone. I soon discovered that my caution had registered—in the most creative way possible.

When I came back, I found my four-year-old had put on my husband's adult-sized shorts—the denim hanging all the way down to her tiny ankles, and a big pillow strategically placed between her shorts and bottom. At the sight of her plumped up, cushy seat and the look of complete satisfaction on her face, there was no way I could squelch my laughter. As if that wasn't enough to disarm me completely, she smiled with the confidence of a tiny negotiator and said, "Mommy, don't worry. Be happy."

I stood there for several seconds, staring at her—speechless and dumbfounded. The scene was so comical that before I could catch myself, I burst into laughter again, my attempt at discipline completely unraveling. And that was it. Although I disciplined my children when it was necessary, that was one instance where I was not able to follow through.

In our home, discipline wasn't a momentary event—I wanted it to be a journey of exploration from mistake to understanding. More than behavior modification, it was heart work. The goal was never just obedient children, but developing empathetic humans who understood the ripple effects of their choices.

Back then, when the gentle impact from a wooden spoon had done its work, we'd find a quiet corner where the real heart-shaping began. They'd sit across from me, small shoulders tensed, waiting for the talk they sometimes dreaded more than the physical punishment. The conversations gently probed beyond actions to the attitudes behind them.

My lead-in was: "How would you feel if someone did that to you?" The question often hung in the air while emotions worked across their young faces. Defiance softened into reflection, and sometimes, I got to see that precious moment when empathy flickered to life in their eyes. Their answers came hesitantly at first—explanations, excuses, then occasionally the truth. These talks aimed to excavate beyond behavior to the heart's hidden places, helping my children see the invisible threads that tie our actions to others' feelings.

I'm not sure which they disliked more—the momentary sting of the paddle or these heart-excavating talks that required them to look inward. But without understanding, discipline would only breed resentment, not growth. The blueprint for these moments wasn't drawn from parenting books but traced from the light and shadows of my own growing years. Some inherited patterns needed gentle revision, others required complete redesign. The architecture of discipline in our home was carefully constructed, attempting to build respect without fear as the foundation, boundaries with clear pathways back to belonging, and consequences that always, always led back to love.

My goal was always reconciliation and unconditional love despite mistakes. At first, they'd keep their distance—wounded, defensive, or ashamed. But as we talked through what happened, I'd watch their posture soften. Eventually, they'd come to me for a hug, their little bodies melting into mine. These physical surrenders mirrored the emotional passage from resistance to acceptance. By the time we pulled ourselves apart, I hoped healing had happened in that space between correction and connection—a quiet promise that nothing, not even the worst mistakes, could diminish my love for them.

That afternoon, watching my four-year-old stand there with her pillow-padded behind and that "don't worry, be happy" smile, my laughter taught us both something I hadn't expected. *Who could keep a straight face at such innocent cleverness?*

I'd planned to teach her about consequences that day, but instead, we both discovered that love has room for both discipline and delight. We discovered that creativity and humor have a place, even in serious situations. More importantly, we glimpsed a truth about God's heart—that even in the midst of our messes, He still celebrates who we are.

Parenting is humbling work, isn't it? Looking back, I see the beautiful mess of it all—days when patience flowed like honey and others when bedtime couldn't come fast enough. Now I watch my grown daughters with their kids, handling situations with wisdom that makes me think, "Wow, where'd you learn that trick?" (Certainly not from me!) We've had our heart-to-hearts about the past. I've joked that I could recommend a colleague who might offer a "buy one, get two free" family discount if they ever needed to "process" their childhood.

This stumbling trek through parenthood has taught me something profound about God—His love transcends our mistakes. My heart has always reached for connection with my children, through tantrums and triumphs alike. How much more does our heavenly Father pursue a close relationship with us?

This perspective on parenting made me reconsider how I read Scripture, too. What if we've been reading the Old Testament all wrong? Often remembered more for fire and brimstone than for what fills most of its pages, a love story of divine persistence, the Old Testament of the Bible shows us we are treasured. In today's language, God would be that faithful partner who keeps showing up despite being ghosted, stood up, and betrayed—time and time again.

Look at the myriad examples. The flood waters rising. Sodom in flames. Plagues descending on Egypt. These make for riveting Sunday School flannel boards and supposedly "great"—though actually terrifying—children's story books. But focusing on the drama means missing something crucial—God's extraordinary patience before those moments. It's like reading only the final chapter of a novel.

What we don't often see are the countless divine attempts God makes at reconciliation. He whispers invitations to return, His outstretched hands are repeatedly slapped away, we see the heart of a Creator grieving as His creation spirals further from Him. Scripture gives us glimpses of His divine patience, but rarely the full backstory of how many times God pursued before consequences finally came. Reading through Judges feels like watching a parent give warning after warning, only to have a child repeatedly touch the hot stove anyway. The burns that follow aren't punishment—they're the natural consequence of ignoring wisdom offered in love.

What would change about your faith if you saw the Old Testament as less about judgment and more about relentless love? Like a parent who's warned a child twenty times about touching a hot stove, God's disciplinary actions were never His first response—they were His reluctant last resort.

The story of Adam and Eve pulls back the curtain on this divine heart from the beginning. Picture it. The fruit has been eaten. The damage done. Most of us would storm into the garden demanding explanations, perhaps with eviction notices in hand. But what does God do? He takes an evening stroll, calling for them as He always had. "Adam? Where are you?"

Perhaps God hoped they would come forward and confess what they had done. Even as they hid in shame and guilt, God called Adam by name—gently inquiring, a gracious gesture signifying a close, personal relationship and His desire for continued dialogue. The question echoed through the garden—not because God didn't know, but because He wanted Adam and Eve to recognize where they were: hiding, afraid, ashamed.

Shame and guilt—emotions never cast upon them by God—had made strangers of them to themselves and to Him. In a tender act of grace, it is God who approached them gently, removing their irritating, self-made garments of fig leaves, and dressing them in garments crafted to cover their shame. The Lord sacrificed animals He had created in order to make the new garments for Adam and Eve, displaying the seriousness of His heart's cry for reconciliation. Through this gesture, God demonstrated His commitment to mending what was broken and reaffirmed their relationship, embodying a love that seeks restoration, regardless of the paths we take.

In the face of our own imperfections, there is comfort in knowing that God's divine compassion constantly envelopes us, even when we feel most distant. This enduring love invites us to step out from our hiding places, to embrace being covered by grace rather than shame. May we always remember that restoration is not just a possibility but a promise—born from a deep love that seeks to draw us closer.

In our own lives, how often do we shy away from connection due to shame or guilt? Could embracing vulnerability allow us to experience reunification with God and healing in our spirits? What self-made barriers, like metaphorical fig leaves or pillow-padding, do we hold onto? How might releasing them invite transformative love into our relationships? How would cultivating grace and forgiveness change not only our own hearts but also deepen our bonds?

> May we always remember that restoration is not just a possibility but a promise— born from a deep love that seeks to draw us closer.

The journey from hiding to healing begins with answering a simple question that echoes through every human heart. *Where are you?* When we are honest enough to admit where we are, brave enough to step out and face our Father—despite our sin, our mistakes, our shame—we discover the transformative power of transparency.

Unlike my clever daughter with her pillow padding, we don't need protective barriers to come before God when we feel we have failed Him. We need courage. Raw, trembling courage to drop our

When we are honest enough to admit where we are, brave enough to step out and face our Father—despite our sin, our mistakes, our shame—we discover the transformative power of transparency.

fig leaves. To stand exposed in all our imperfection. To walk toward love instead of away from it.

God isn't waiting with a paddle. He's waiting with open arms.

In those moments of brave surrender—when we finally exhale the breath we've been holding since Eden—we discover what we've been searching for through every human connection: not escape from our failures, but the healing embrace of a Father who treasures relationship over rules.

What my four-year-old understood instinctively, I still struggle to believe. Even when I've broken the rules, God still finds me loveable. His heart doesn't harden when I fail. It softens at my return.

And in that melting moment, something shifts inside us. The desire to hide transforms into a longing to please—not from fear of punishment, but from the unshakable knowledge that we are loved beyond reason. My daughter's, "Don't worry, be happy," wasn't just childhood charm—it was profound theology wrapped in pigtails and pillow padding.

God's question has never been "What have you done?" but always "Where are you?" He doesn't ask because He's lost us. He asks because He wants us to realize where we are—one step away from accepting His grace.

Father,

How often I've played this ancient game of hiding when I have sinned, when shame clings to me like heavy robes, when I fear that my flaws make me unworthy of love. I have hidden behind busyness, behind perfectionism, behind the hope that invisibility might spare me from the ache of my own brokenness.

Yet, Your question still echoes, "Where are you?"

Lord, give me the courage to answer when You call my name. Infuse me with the strength to step out from behind the trees, to stand vulnerable before You, to whisper, "Here I am."

Your question invites, not accuses. Your tone is love, not wrath.

In moments when shame whispers that I should run from Your presence, remind me of Your garden walks—how You've always moved toward me, never away. When I struggle to believe I'm worth pursuing, remind me of the road You walked for me—the pain you endured, the shame you bore, the love poured out in Your precious blood.

Open my hands to release the fig leaves. Help me to stand before You—unhidden, unafraid, utterly known. For what parent doesn't treasure the unfiltered honesty of their child above all pretense?

And in all my relationships, Lord, let me mirror your grace. Help me create spaces where others can step out from their hiding places, where reconciliation replaces retribution. Where vulnerability is met with tenderness. Where love does not demand perfection but embraces honesty.

May I grasp in the core of my being, the width, length, height and depth of a love that never changes.

In Jesus' name. Amen.

A Moment of Reflection

1. What childhood understanding of God's nature still influences your adult spirituality?

____

____

____

____

2. When was the last time you experienced grace instead of the judgment you expected? How did that moment reshape your understanding of love?

____

____

____

____

3. What "fig leaves" are you hiding behind right now? What are you protecting yourself from being seen or known?

____

____

____

____

4. *Think about a specific relationship where shame, fear, or guilt has caused you to retreat. What would it take for you to step out from behind that barrier?*

____

____

____

____

5. *In what areas of your life are you listening for accusation when God is actually asking, "Where are you?" with the voice of someone seeking connection?*

____

____

____

____

6. *In your relationship with God or with others, where have rules taken priority over reconciliation? What would it look like to shift that focus?*

____

____

____

____

9

"Your Receiver is Broken"

Opening our hands to receive can feel infinitely harder than extending them to give. Some of us eagerly help others while shrinking back from vulnerability when we ourselves have a need. True healing begins when we recognize that our "receiver" may be broken—silently blocking the very support we desperately need. Learning to accept help is as much a spiritual journey as learning to provide it.

> Learning to accept help is as much a spiritual journey as learning to provide it.

> *But Ruth replied, "Don't urge me to leave you or to turn back from you. Where you go I will go, and where you stay I will stay. Your people will be my people and your God my God. Where you die I will die, and there I will be buried. May the LORD deal with me, be it*

*ever so severely, if even death separates you and me."
When Naomi realized that Ruth was determined to go
with her, she stopped urging her.*

*So the two women went on until they came to Bethle-
hem. When they arrived in Bethlehem, the whole town
was stirred because of them, and the women exclaimed,
"Can this be Naomi?"*

*"Don't call me Naomi," she told them. "Call me Mara, be-
cause the Almighty has made my life very bitter. I went
away full, but the Lord has brought me back empty. Why
call me Naomi? The Lord has afflicted me; the Almighty
has brought misfortune upon me." So Naomi returned
from Moab accompanied by Ruth the Moabite, her
daughter-in-law, arriving in Bethlehem as the barley
harvest was beginning.*

RUTH 1:16–22 (NIV)

"Your receiver is broken."

"What?"

"Your receiver is broken," she said, her face etched with concern.

I stood there frozen, caught by surprise in the spotlight of a truth I wasn't sure I was ready to face. As a young woman, I had mastered the art of projecting confidence. My carefully constructed façade radiated happiness and self-assurance, but the cracks were beginning to show, visible to those who looked closely enough.

The concrete sidewalks of New Jersey had shaped my childhood, teaching me crucial lessons about staying safe—the importance of being street-smart and staying poised under pressure. Though deep down I was a highly sensitive person, I learned to leave that vulnerable girl behind. I watched early on how sensitive souls, including myself, became easy targets, their emotional openness exploited like an unlocked door. So, like Clark Kent transforming into Superman, I chose to change who I was by transforming into someone that projected self-sufficiency and confidence. This image would propel me much further in life. I traded transparency for a cape of calculated strength.

My mature demeanor, like a too-large coat I grew into before its time, invited responsibilities beyond my years. It was ironic. In some ways, I was overprotected, yet in others, I was given adult responsibilities far too early. My physical appearance—older than my chronological age—only reinforced this misconception. While I carried myself as someone who could shoulder the weight of the world, my emotional capacity remained that of a young girl, stretched thin across expectations I hadn't chosen.

Now, I found myself at a point in my life where my support system had dissolved, and I was struggling to keep my head above water. The weight of being alone was becoming unbearable. I desperately needed guidance, and thankfully, my friend was there to offer it.

"What do you mean my receiver is broken?" I asked, my voice catching slightly on the words. The question hung between us, an admission that perhaps she could see something I couldn't.

She looked at me steadily and sighed, "You rush to give, dropping everything to help anyone with a need, yet when it comes to receiving, you're guarded. I want to give you what you need, but you push me away, acting like you've got it all figured out on your own."

Her words struck home, penetrating deeper than I wanted to admit. For years, I had poured myself out like water for others, finding purpose in being the healer, the supporter, the strong one. Yet, my own past wounds were hidden behind a locked heart, making it challenging to admit my needs and allow people to come close enough to see my pain.

Transparency felt daunting, like letting someone see the unedited pages of my journal. But I soon learned that healing only happens in the context of vulnerability. Through this friendship, God was offering me a place where I could lay down my armor. A space where I could fully exhale, perhaps for the first time. The invitation to safety where I could finally heal stood before me. She was offering me real friendship, the kind where I didn't have to pretend. I just needed the courage to say yes.

> Healing only happens in the context of vulnerability.

Healing begins with acknowledgment—in the moment when we stop denying our brokenness and accept the helping hands extended toward us. Just as a patient must recognize their illness before treatment can begin, we must embrace our vulnerability. This means sharing our deepest feelings and needs within the safe relationships that God provides, allowing others to walk alongside us as we make our way toward wholeness.

> Healing begins with acknowledgment—in the moment when we stop denying our brokenness and accept the helping hands extended toward us.

In the book of Ruth, we encounter Naomi, a woman overwhelmed by heartache. Having lost everything while dwelling in a foreign land, she trudges back to her homeland, the weight of emptiness heavy on her shoulders. Upon arrival, she doesn't hide behind pleasantries or minimize her pain. Instead, she gives voice to how her suffering has altered her very identity.

The name "Naomi," meaning "pleasant" or "delight," no longer reflected the woman standing before neighbors and friends. "Call me Mara," she insisted, choosing a name that meant "bitter" to reflect the deep anguish she felt inside. Her raw honesty created space and opened the door for healing to take place. As the story continues, both Naomi and Ruth humbly positioned themselves to receive protection and kindness from their kinsman, Boaz. Their willingness to express vulnerability and accept help led to a beautiful story of redemption.

Throughout the changing seasons of our lives, God strategically places people who become vessels of restoration. Healing flows when we position ourselves to receive what they offer. Past wounds often lead us to build walls around our hearts for protection, yet these divinely orchestrated relationships invite us to lower those defenses. Like Naomi, being honest about sharing our genuine reality creates space for receiving the support extended to us.

God values truthfulness—not just in what we tell others, but in what we admit to ourselves. When we embrace full honesty, peeling back layers of pretense to reveal our authentic selves, we create pathways for deeper connection. By acknowledging our limitations and opening our hearts to others, we create sacred space for God's love to flow through the people He sends our way. In our moments of greatest

> When we embrace full honesty, peeling back layers of pretense to reveal our authentic selves, we create pathways for deeper connection.

humility, we often discover unexpected strength and grace, experiencing the beauty that emerges when we allow our healing to be a collaborative work rather than a solitary burden.

Remember, the Lord can use anyone—friend, family, even a stranger—as a vessel through which comfort flows. These divine appointments bring support, guidance, and wisdom, often in ways we never anticipated. Trust His orchestration of these connections, and when they appear, let your receiver be open to the blessings they bring.

Dear Heavenly Father,

I come before You with open hands and a heart longing to be free from the burdens I've carried too long. You see where my walls of self-sufficiency have been built—brick by brick—out of fear and hurt. You know how I've guarded myself, even from the help You've lovingly placed before me. Lord, I confess that my "receiver" has been broken, blocking the blessings You've sent my way.

Send people into my life, Father—real people who can offer Your love and restoration. Help me recognize them, trust them, and open my heart to what they have to give. Give me the courage to let down my defenses, to lay aside the armor I no longer need.

Lord, show me how to position myself to receive—not just from those around me, but from You. Remind me that true strength grows in humility and that healing begins when I dare to acknowledge my brokenness.

Break down the barriers that keep me from experiencing the fullness of Your grace and the beauty of collaborative healing. Help me to see that I am never alone and that Your hands are always reaching toward me through others.

Like Naomi, I name my pain. I bring my bitterness, my fear, and my weakness before You. But I also name my hope. You are the Redeemer who weaves beauty from brokenness and turns sorrow into joy. I long for Your healing touch.

In Jesus' name, Amen.

A Moment of Reflection

1. In what ways have you built "walls of self-sufficiency" to protect yourself from vulnerability? What are those walls actually protecting?

____

____

____

____

2. Think about a time when someone offered you genuine support, but you pushed them away or minimized your need. What was happening inside you in that moment?

____

____

____

3. When you look back at your younger self, what messages did you absorb about needing help or showing weakness? How might those early lessons still be shaping you today?

____

____

____

____

4. *When you rush to help others but resist receiving help yourself, what does that pattern allow you to avoid feeling or facing?*

____

____

____

____

5. *If you let down your armor and allowed someone to truly see your pain, what's the worst thing you believe might happen?*

____

____

____

____

6. *Naomi didn't hide behind pleasantries—she named her bitterness out loud. What would you need to name honestly, without minimizing or explaining it away, to create space for your own healing?*

____

____

____

10

Undivided Attention

Her voice came through the phone, breathless from moving boxes. I hesitated, knowing she was drowning in chaos, but the next sixty seconds revealed the most beautiful truth about divine attention—your prayers summon His pause.

> *The eyes of the Lord are toward the righteous [those*
> *with moral courage and spiritual integrity]*
> *And his ears are open to their cry.*
>
> PSALM 34:15 (AMP)

The day had been brimming with action, and now the afternoon sunlight started to cast its golden glow across the horizon, touching everything with its warmth. Caught up in a whirlwind of preparations, I was gearing up for my upcoming adventure—a mission to lead a devoted team on an international ministry expedition spanning several weeks.

With every tick of the clock our departure drew closer, sparking an exhilarating urgency inside me. Time seemed to rush away, slipping through my fingers like grains of sand in a tightly held hourglass. A whirlwind of thoughts clouded my mind, leaving me overwhelmed.

In a moment of anxious desperation, I reached for my phone to call my friend. She was knee-deep in the chaos of moving, but I hoped that just a few minutes of her wisdom would anchor my scattered thoughts. We were coordinating this trip together, and I needed her insight to process the remaining tasks hovering over me.

"Hello?" her voice came through the phone, breathless and momentarily strained.

"Chari? I'm sorry to bother you with all these details in the middle of everything you have to do, but—" I stopped mid-sentence, hearing the unmistakable crinkle of bubble wrap and the scrape of cardboard against hardwood in the background.

"No, no, it's fine! I can talk," she insisted, the sound of packing tape ripping punctuating her words. "What's going on?"

"I'll make it quick, I promise." Relief washed over me as I spilled my concerns, words tumbling out rapidly in compressed sentences to minimize my intrusion on her time. "The departure date is coming up fast and I still need to coordinate the team's accommodations, finalize my messages, and figure out . . ."

As I stumbled over my words, she interrupted me with her gentle, calming voice, "I am here. I stopped what I was doing, and I am listening. You have my full attention. I walked into the other room, where it is empty, and I am laying on the floor, fully focused on what you need."

Amidst her half-unpacked life, surrounded by towers of cardboard waiting to be emptied, Chari had paused everything to concentrate entirely on what I needed. Her unexpected attentiveness stunned me into stillness. Her simple action brought those words to life in a way I'd never understood before. *The eyes of the Lord are on the righteous, and his ears are attentive to their cry.* That's exactly what my friend had just done for me.

The pressure valve inside me released. No longer feeling hurried or pressured, I deliberately slowed my words down, giving them space to uncoil naturally. I stopped rushing to get them out quickly so that she could move on to her list of tasks at hand. The nagging sensation of being an interruption faded and the weight of being a burden was lifted from my shoulders. Her gentle words wrapped around me like a warm blanket on a winter night, soothing my frayed nerves and bringing me a deep sense of peace. In that moment I felt seen, heard, and understood.

Beyond immediate comfort, Chari's response unveiled a profound truth God had been waiting for me to discover. When I speak to God, I have his full, undivided attention. He is never distracted or half-hearted in His listening, Instinctively, His heart gravitates towards mine, where I can experience His love and Presence. Even in my most scattered moments, nothing exists in the universe more important to Him than my words.

> Even in my most scattered moments, nothing exists in the universe more important to Him than my words.

There is nothing in your life—no concern too small, no burden too heavy—that you cannot carry to your Heavenly Father. Like my friend on that busy day, He stops everything to listen with a focused ear—because nothing is more important to Him than loving on you.

Heavenly Father,

In this quiet moment, I come to You with all my messy thoughts and unspoken needs. It's mind boggling to think that You—Creator of Everything—stop to listen when I speak.

Nothing is more important to Him than loving on you.

You see me when I struggle to find words, when tears are my only language, when confusion clouds my mind. You don't turn away. You don't check the time. You don't wish I'd hurry up and get to the point.

The moment I pray, You hear my stumbling prayers as if they were the only sounds in Your universe. My words matter to You. My pain matters to You. My joy matters to You.

Help me sink into this truth like a warm embrace. I am never an interruption to You. Teach me to drop everything for others as You do for me—to listen with my whole heart when someone needs to be heard.

Thank You for drawing near when I feel most scattered, calming my emotions and giving me the clarity I need to move forward when I don't know what to do. May this sacred pause between us be my refuge in every challenge I face.

In Jesus' name, Amen.

A Moment of Reflection

1. *I called my friend despite knowing she was "knee-deep in the chaos of moving." What barriers keep you from reaching out to the support system God has placed in your life?*

____

____

____

____

2. *How might pride or self-sufficiency be masking themselves as consideration for others?*

____

____

____

____

3. *What childhood messages or experiences might have taught you that your needs were "too much" or "a bother"? How has this affected your relationships?*

____

____

____

4. *In what areas of your life do you minimize your own needs to avoid feeling like a burden?*

____

____

____

____

5. *Independence can become an idol that separates us from God's design for community. When has your self-sufficiency actually hindered your spiritual growth rather than helped it?*

____

____

____

____

6. *What do you do when you feel overwhelmed? Do you look for someone (God or other relationship) who can stabilize you? Or do you look for something to escape into?*

____

____

____

____

11

Beautifully Flawed

___

We carry within us a longing to be seen, truly seen, and found beautiful despite our blemishes. Yet how often do our eyes—and the eyes of others—become magnets for imperfection, drawn to the one flaw that mars an otherwise perfect moment? The heart of our Father beats to a different rhythm entirely—He sees beauty, not blemishes, potential not problems.

> *"'I will get up and go to my father, and I will say to him "Father, I have sinned against heaven and in your sight. I am no longer worthy to be called your son; [just] treat me like one of your hired men."' So he got up and came to his father. But while he was still a long way off, his father saw him and was moved with compassion for him, and ran and embraced him and kissed him."*
>
> LUKE 15:18–20 (AMP)

"Look at me Papi! Do you like my new dress?"

At four years old, I loved twirling and parading before Papi in my new dresses. My father possessed a deep appreciation for beauty—a grandchild's laughter, the majesty of the ocean, my mother's natural charm and grace. Though he was usually a very serious man, in those moments, laughter would escape from him. "Ay, que linda! You look beautiful," he would say. Those words wrapped around me like a warm embrace, making me feel truly seen and loved.

One of my favorite things about him was his greeting. Whether it was the doorbell ringing ten times in a row or his voice booming through the entryway, he didn't just enter the room—he filled it. Some of us inherited that grand entrance, much to our family's fond exasperation. Eyes would roll, but then the smiles would sneak out.

I remember the day he made the hour-long trip to my house. When I heard his car pulling up the driveway, I ran out toward him with excitement. I flung open his car door and leaned in for our traditional greeting—that swift, sweet kiss that said "I love you" without words.

But before my lips could find his cheek, he paused. "There's a pimple on your nose."

I can laugh at the memory now, but in that moment, surprise and embarrassment washed over me. Words abandoned me entirely. In an instant, the joy that had brought me running across the driveway dissolved, and a wave of aggravation and sadness took its place, robbing my moment of happiness and replacing it with shame. In my eagerness to greet my father, I had forgotten what had greeted me first thing in the morning when I looked in the mirror. A blemish too big to hide, sat right on the tip of my nose. I had failed the beauty inspection without even knowing I was being tested.

That day, my father missed the overwhelming joy and excitement I felt as I ran to greet him with love. A single pimple on my nose grabbed his attention, causing him to miss a heartfelt connection that could have been treasured by both our hearts.

How often are our eyes instinctively drawn to focus on the one fault, the single weakness, instead of seeing the whole beautiful person standing before us? How many connections do we miss while hunting for imperfections?

Years later, God gifted me with a friend whose wisdom felt comforting, while her pursuit of excellence reminded me of my upbringing. She exhibited that familiar dance of high standards and careful observation. One afternoon, discouraged and raw, I confessed my fear of disappointing her. "I'm afraid I'll fail you," I whispered, "because perfect is something I'll never be."

Her response surprised me. "I'm not looking for perfect. I like you just the way you are."

Those words freed me. Her acceptance of my failures and flaws breathed hope back into my heart, releasing me from the belief that imperfection meant ugliness. We began calling ourselves "beautifully flawed," and somehow that phrase held more truth than any compliment ever had.

It's so easy to focus on how something could have been said differently, allowing a single mistake to grab all our attention. Like that glaring pimple on an otherwise perfect reunion, one shortcoming can steal the spotlight from all that is good and true. In those moments, we miss opportunities to recognize beauty, to speak words that could brighten someone's entire day.

As someone who values excellence, I've had to retrain my eyes— they were educated to hunt for flaws, but I'm teaching them to hunt for beauty instead. I've chosen to seek out the positives instead of being distracted by the negatives.

So, in pondering that memory I ask myself: when does the pursuit of excellence slip into perfectionism? Maybe it's when we trade love's wide lens for a magnifying glass. Excellence embraces the whole canvas; perfectionism fixates on the flaw.

Genuine love means accepting both the beautiful and the broken parts of ourselves and others. When people bring me their complaints about others, I often ask, "But there are things about them you truly love, right? You have to realize it's a package deal. You can't edit out someone's flaws, their struggles and keep only their strengths."

> Genuine love means accepting both the beautiful and the broken parts of ourselves and others.

By accepting imperfections, both in ourselves and in others, we can cultivate relationships that are deeper and more genuine. We find safety in being known completely, and loved anyway. A change in perspective will enrich our lives and allow us to truly appreciate the people we care about, embracing them in their entirety.

The Bible overflows with stories of beautifully flawed people—men and women whose weaknesses were written in permanent ink yet whose hearts God treasured. King David, who carried the dual weight of adultery and murder on his conscience. Peter, whose fear made him deny the very One he loved most. The prodigal son, who traded his inheritance for empty pleasures and pig slop. Stories such as these demonstrate that God is a Father full of grace who forgives, redeems, and embraces us, despite our shortcomings and mistakes. He is the God who discounts our failures and multiplies our chances.

> He is the God who discounts our failures and multiplies our chances.

Like my friend's unconditional acceptance of me, God desires a relationship with us, valuing connection over perfection. Our Father sees us with eyes that focus not on our blemishes but on our beauty. He is the Father who runs—who sees us from a distance and comes toward us, arms wide, heart full.

I think about that little girl in the new dress sometimes, spinning with such confidence in her father's love. She didn't know she needed to be perfect to be loved—she just knew she was adored. Maybe that's the secret. Returning to that place of simple trust, where we run toward our Father, not because we've finally gotten it all right, but because we know He's running toward us, too.

The next time you catch yourself focusing on someone's pimple, or your own, remember that God's eyes work differently than ours. He doesn't embrace us because we're perfect; He runs toward us because we're His. In a world obsessed with pristine selfies and impossible standards, we get to live as beautifully flawed children of a Father who sees our hearts, not our blemishes. That's not just good news. That's freedom.

> Our Father sees us with eyes that focus not on our blemishes but on our beauty.

Father,

Thank You for seeing me through eyes of love, not judgment. You are the God who sees my heart when all I can see are my failures. Like that little girl spinning in her new dress, let me remember the joy of simply being loved by You.

Forgive me for the times I've focused on people's flaws instead of celebrating their beauty. When my eyes become magnets for imperfection, redirect them toward Your grace. Teach my eyes to see as You see beauty in brokenness, potential in imperfection, love where I might only notice blemishes.

When perfectionism whispers that I must earn Your acceptance, quiet that voice with the truth of Your unconditional love. Help me live from the freedom of knowing I'm already chosen, already cherished, already enough in Your sight.

God of countless chances, thank You for running toward me while I'm still a long way off. Give me the courage to run toward You too—not because I've gotten everything right, but because I know You're waiting for me.

May I carry Your heart into every relationship, choosing to see the whole picture instead of zooming in on the cracks. Help me be a safe place for others to be beautifully flawed, just as You are for me.

In the name of Jesus, who loves me perfectly imperfect. Amen.

A Moment of Reflection

1. *Where in your life are you performing for approval rather than resting in acceptance?*

2. *What would you do if you weren't afraid of failing or not being "good enough"?*

3. *What "pimples" do you fixate on when you look at yourself—physically, emotionally, spiritually? How might God see those same areas differently?*

4. *Think about someone close to you. What flaw or imperfection tends to grab your attention and steal your focus from all that's beautiful about them?*

____

____

____

____

5. *If perfectionism is a thief, what has it stolen from you? What joy, peace, or connection have you lost while hunting for flaws?*

____

____

____

____

6. *What wound from your childhood still determines how you see yourself today? What would it take for you to finally let that voice go and believe you're loved exactly as you are?*

____

____

____

____

12

The Savoring Sigh

Some days arrive wrapped in chaos, each hour unraveling our carefully laid plans until we're left wondering where the time went. Yet sometimes, within those very moments we least expect, grace shows up at our doorstep with gifts we never saw coming.

> *God looked over everything he had made;*
> *it was so good, so very good!*
>
> GENESIS 1:31 (MSG)

You know those days when nothing goes according to plan? The kind where you're juggling appointments that lead nowhere, and feeling like you're constantly one step behind? This was certainly one of those—a day full of unexpected turns. My husband and I had gone to a virtually useless appointment, a mere detour that sent us on a wild goose chase to another office, where we waited endlessly, just to schedule yet another appointment, while the time I had hoped to spend with my granddaughter slipped away.

To add to our day, my daughter and her family faced an unforeseen flat tire on the highway. Although I was thankful for their safety, my mother's heart was feeling the stress she was experiencing. On top of this, my other plans to enjoy an afternoon with my friend seemed to slip further from reach. I called her and she reassured me she would stop by to connect briefly, anyway. Christmas was just a week away, and my to-do list seemed to grow longer by the hour. We were truly "grabbing a moment."

Needless to say, I was running on fumes and frustration when my friend knocked on the door. As it turned out, the "moment" unfolded into a very special one, as my friend walked in with presents for me. But instead of happiness flooding through me, heat crept up my neck as I stood there empty-handed, stammering apologies. "Oh my gosh!" I am so sorry! With Jim being sick, time got away from me and I didn't have time to shop for the special present I wanted to give you," I said.

My humiliation quickly gave way to relief. My friend responded with nothing but grace and understanding. "Please allow me the blessing of being a giver," she said.

My joy grew as I saw all the presents, each one individually wrapped carefully and with love. Every gift had been chosen for me with great intention and with heartfelt emotion. As if that weren't enough, her brother, whom I hadn't seen in years, sent me a gift along with a personalized poem he wrote especially for me. Each line of his poem brought tears to my eyes, touching my heart, bridging years of separation, built word by word. Laughter and warmth settled over us as wrapping paper crinkled underfoot.

My husband, always the gracious host, warmly served us with rich espresso, paired with the freshly baked cookies I had previously prepared. Christmas lights and Christmas decorations adorned my living room, and my friend complimented all I had done to make the environment warm and enjoyable. The friendship and love coming from our deep-rooted connection, something we had nurtured for more than 20 years, wrapped around us like a well-worn quilt, stitched with years of shared memories. The challenges we had walked through together and all the work we had done to build a strong relationship culminated in the space of this one glorious moment.

Time slipped away like sand through our fingers, and suddenly we were shocked to realize how late it was. We had to acknowledge it, despite our reluctance. As my friend started to get up, she let out a long sigh.

Trying to be humorous, I asked her if she was yawning.

She responded, "It's a sigh of satisfaction."

I had experienced a lot of sighs in my life, but never a positive one. Later that day, reflecting on our time together, I found myself smiling. Some sighs express exasperation; others release pure satisfaction. My friend showed her contentment and joy.

I love the way God shows us that He experiences feelings and expresses them the way we do. In Mark 7:34 there's a reference to Jesus' sighing. However, my friend's sigh reminded me of the moments described in Genesis 1 when God brought order to the earth, separating the seas and the lands, and again at the end of each day of creation. Satisfied, He looked upon all He had accomplished and savored it. God was satisfied and Genesis 1 says over and over, "And God said, it is good."

I wonder, why don't we stop more often to capture moments of God's blessings with a satisfying sigh? My friend created a memory we could both savor, tuck into our hearts, and carry into the future. Memory is God's way of letting us live the good parts more than once. Savoring precious memories serves a meaningful purpose.

Scientists are actually discovering that revisiting happy memories does more than just make us smile. Research confirms that when we intentionally recall positive experiences, our brains respond as if we're

> Studies find that people who regularly practice this kind of "memory savoring" report higher levels of happiness and show greater resilience when facing new challenges.

living them again, releasing the same feel-good chemicals and even lowering stress hormones like cortisol. It's like having a built-in therapy session whenever we need it. Studies find that people who regularly practice this kind of "memory savoring" report higher levels of happiness and show greater resilience when facing new challenges. So, when we pause to remember the good times, we're not just being nostalgic—we're actually strengthening our capacity for joy.

In difficult times, they help us move through challenges, providing the strength to persevere. By revisiting happy moments, we anchor ourselves, transforming sadness into contentment and satisfaction, fostering resilience and elevating our spirits with hope.

Who knew that grabbing a moment with my friend would turn a challenging day into a treasured memory? Now when I think back, I vividly recall the Christmas lights twinkling in the background. I remember the tissue paper as I unwrapped the presents. I see her radiant smile and the sparkle in her eyes.

I can still feel the warmth of that afternoon. I remember how my friend's unexpected sigh taught me to recognize the sacred in the ordinary, to pause and breathe in the goodness that surrounds us even on the hardest days. God doesn't just create beautiful moments—He savors them, and He invites us to do the same.

So, I'm learning to pause too, to breathe in the sweetness of unexpected gifts, and to let my own contented sigh rise like a prayer of gratitude. You might be surprised by what you discover when you stop rushing long enough to taste the sweetness of where you are.

Dear God,

Thank You for the way You transform chaos into peace, shame into grace, and ordinary moments into treasured memories. For showing me through my friend's visit that Your goodness often arrives when we least expect it.

By revisiting happy moments, we anchor ourselves, transforming sadness into contentment and satisfaction, fostering resilience and elevating our spirits with hope.

Help me to pause.

To notice. To breathe in the sacred moments You weave into the fabric of ordinary days. When chaos threatens to steal my peace, remind me that You are present, working Your grace in ways I can discover if I look for it.

Teach me to savor, Lord. To hold the good memories close, not as escapes from reality, but as anchors of hope. Let me learn from Your example—how You looked upon all You made and called it very good.

When life overwhelms and plans crumble, let me remember that You are still weaving grace into my story. You're writing something more beautiful than I can imagine.

Give me a heart that recognizes Your blessings, even when they arrive wrapped in ways I didn't expect. Help me be a gift to others, just as my friend was to me that day.

And in the quiet moments of reflection, when memories surface like treasures, let my gratitude reach You in the quietness.

Thank You for the gift of living good memories more than once, each one deepening my gratitude.

In Jesus' name, Amen.

A Moment of Reflection

1. *How do you typically respond when your carefully laid plans crumble? What does that response reveal about what you're really holding onto?*

2. *Think of a recent moment that brought you deep satisfaction. When you replay it in your mind, what do you notice that you might have missed in the rush of living it?*

3. *Where in your life right now are you moving too fast to notice the sweetness that's already there?*

4. *Think about the last time someone gave you an unexpected gift or showed you grace when you felt empty-handed. What made it hard to simply receive?*

____

____

____

____

5. *When you feel you have "nothing to give back" in a relationship or situation, what story do you tell yourself about your worth?*

____

____

____

____

6. *What are you afraid you'll miss or lose if you slow down long enough to savor where you are right now?*

____

____

____

____

13

Extravagant Love

Some of my most painful childhood memories sit right next to my most joyful ones, separated only by the thin veil of time and perspective. Learning to find God in both the heartbreak and the celebration has become one of my greatest spiritual discoveries. One Christmas morning revealed that divine love looks nothing like our careful, measured expectations—it's wild, abundant, and breathtakingly generous.

> *I will worship you, YAHWEH, with extended hands as my whole heart erupts with praise! I will tell everyone everywhere about your wonderful works!*
>
> PSALM 9:1 (TPT)

"Babies should come with a manual," I whispered to my premature daughter, both of us terrified.

At twenty-one, staring at this beautiful, tiny human I was somehow supposed to keep alive, that thought felt like a desperate prayer. I remember bringing her home from the hospital and standing frozen in our living room, completely overwhelmed by the weight of responsibility. *What do I do with her now?*

And so began our lifelong journey together—learning what it means to be human. Seriously, I needed a full-length instruction manual, with an appendix, *and* a glossary.

For two days, I dutifully prepared my baby's bottles. She'd take one sip, scrunch her face like I'd given her pickle juice, and wail like I was torturing her. I genuinely thought she was just a particularly fussy baby until my mom walked in, watched me pull out that bottle of liquid winter and winced.

"Mija, you have to warm it up." The look in my mother's wide eyes said everything. I'm sure she was thinking, *Oh no, what have we done? This baby's future is in her hands.*

Bathtime wasn't much better. The moment my child's tiny body touched the water, she'd unleash a scream that could wake the entire neighborhood, then hold her breath until her face turned an alarming shade of purple. Panicked, I'd blow directly into her face—puff, puff—like some kind of desperate CPR technique, just to get her breathing again. Was the water too cold? Too hot? Too wet? I had no idea.

Our first child, sad to say, became our guinea pig for learning how to keep a human alive. Turns out, motherhood doesn't come with instructions—it comes with sleepless nights, steep learning curves, and desperate prayers asking God to make up for your mistakes.

This humbling crash course in parenting taught me something profound about grace: it isn't learned when we're competent, it's revealed in our struggles. When I think about my own parents and their mistakes, I can't help but remember those first terrifying weeks with my daughter.

They were doing their best with what they knew, just like I was fumbling through those early days of motherhood.

My parents were definitely better parents than their parents. They carried the weight of building a life from scratch while trying to raise us—working multiple jobs, navigating systems they didn't fully understand, all while hoping they were making the right choices for our future. Despite the wounds my siblings and I carried from our childhoods, we knew that deep down we were loved. Some days were excruciatingly painful and sad. And then there were days that were unbelievably fun and life-giving.

Holidays in my Colombian household were pure magic—exhilarating and brimming with vibrant life. The air buzzed with energy while the aroma of traditional dishes floated through rooms filled with music that told stories of my parents' homeland. But then came *the* rhythm—you know the one, that beat that reaches into your chest and moves your hips before your brain can object. Suddenly, our living room became a dance floor, there was no fighting it.

Stories flew in rapid-fire Spanish as our relatives laughed at themselves, recalling translating disasters that turned their struggles into comedy gold. They often combined English and Spanish words into a wild hybrid vocabulary. Each tale grew more outrageous, more hilarious, until the whole room exploded with laughter. Little hands tugged at dancing skirts while stories bounced from person to person, children occasionally getting swept up in someone's arms for a spontaneous spin. The joy erupted in waves. One joke triggering another memory, another burst of celebration that seemed to lift the very walls of whatever home we were in. This was the atmosphere of one particular Christmas Eve we spent at a family friend's house.

Instead of slowing down at midnight, the party actually picked up steam. The kids though, were done—drooping eyelids and all. We hunted for any soft surface to collapse on. But that's how we celebrated—as a family, all together. When you work double shifts just to get by, you don't waste weekend moments worrying about bedtimes.

Meanwhile, the adults kept dancing and singing, while the clock ticked unnoticed, until the morning light began peeking through the windows. Our parents carried us, half-asleep, out into the cold New Jersey air to the car, nudging us awake when we arrived home.

Exhausted, my brothers and I shuffled toward our bedroom, dreaming of our own beds—until I caught sight of something out of the corner of my eye. I froze. My eyes flew wide open, and my jaw dropped. Our dining room table had completely vanished beneath a mountainous explosion of presents that looked like a toy store had dumped its entire inventory in our house.

Wild with excitement, we jumped from gift to gift, tearing into each package with complete abandon. Wrapping paper flew around us like confetti, and no one tried to dampen our enthusiasm. Each new toy barely had a moment in the spotlight before we reached for the next treasure. When the last scraps of wrapping paper had been torn away, we stood back and took in the glorious sight: beautiful dolls with their accessories nestled beside board games like *Monopoly* and *Trouble*.

Fire trucks and play rifles sat alongside Indian costumes and cowboy gear—each discovery more thrilling than the last. Just when my eyes couldn't take in anymore, we found even more treasures buried under the pile. It was total madness. Lost in joy, our screeches and squeals filled the air as our parents stood back, their eyes full of pure delight.

Joy has a sound, and that morning it was pure, unbridled shrieking. This is my favorite Christmas memory. That morning, I experienced my parents' love in an extravagant and tangible way. Lavishing love isn't measured—it's abundant.

Years later, as I read the Bible with fresh eyes, I began to see God's extravagant love woven throughout every story. God's love has always been reckless in its abundance.

His generous nature was on full display from the very beginning. In the Garden of Eden, God didn't just meet Adam and Eve's basic needs—He surrounded them with overwhelming beauty and endless possibilities. Fruit trees, heavy with sweetness. Rivers flowing with crystal water. Animals that brought delight rather than fear. When God loves, He doesn't measure portions—He creates paradise.

> His generous nature was on full display from the very beginning. In the Garden of Eden, God didn't just meet Adam and Eve's basic needs—He surrounded them with overwhelming beauty and endless possibilities.

Everything they could have ever needed or desired lay within their grasp. Not because they earned it. Not because they asked for it. But because that's what extravagant love does—it gives abundantly, joyfully, without restraint. Lavishing love isn't careful—it's overwhelming.

The longer I walk with God, the more I realize He's not big on following my carefully laid out plans. I'm so grateful He doesn't.

We map out exactly how life should unfold, complete with timelines and backup strategies. Then God shows up and completely rewrites the script—not to disappoint, but to give us something so much better than our original plans. Our plans? They look like rough drafts next to his masterpiece.

Over and over, the same beautiful truth emerges, our expectations are no match for God's extravagance. We sketch out these neat little plans, thinking we know exactly what we need, and He shows up with gifts so much bigger and better that it leaves us wondering why we ever thought so small. It's like that Christmas morning all over again. It's that same jaw-dropping realization—God's heart is always bigger than our dreams.

God's heart is always bigger than our dreams.

My experience echoes Ephesians 3:20.

The Amplified Bible says it so well:

> *Now to Him who is able to [carry out His purpose and] do superabundantly more than all that we dare ask or think [infinitely beyond our greatest prayers, hopes, or dreams], according to His power that is at work within us, to Him be the glory in the church and in Christ Jesus throughout all generations forever and ever. Amen.*

EPHESIANS 3:20–21

God's love isn't careful, it's extravagant. It doesn't tiptoe; it explodes like wrapping paper flying through the air. It doesn't whisper, it makes us shriek with joy. Because when you're loved by a Father whose heart is extravagant, what seemed impossible becomes inevitable.

Dear Father,

My heart overflows as I remember the ways You've shown Your extravagant love throughout my life. You delight in surprising us with gifts beyond our wildest dreams.

Thank You for the memories that shaped me—even the painful ones that taught me grace. Help me see my own story through Your eyes, recognizing how You were weaving beauty from brokenness, hope from heartache.

Lord, I've painted small pictures of what I thought You should do, only to discover You had grander plans all along. Forgive me for the moments I've doubted Your goodness when things didn't unfold as I expected.

Open my eyes to see Your abundant provision all around me. In the laughter of loved ones, in second chances, in quiet mercies I almost miss— You are constantly pouring out more than I could ask or imagine.

Make me a reflection of Your extravagant heart. Help me love with the same generous spirit, to celebrate others' joy with the delight You take in ours; to offer grace the way You've offered it to me.

In Jesus name, Amen.

A Moment of Reflection

1. **What did love look like in your childhood home? How has that—for better or worse—influenced how you see God's love for you?**

____

____

____

____

2. **Where do you see evidence of God's extravagant love in your life right now that you might be overlooking?**

____

____

____

____

3. **When has God's provision exceeded what you imagined? How did that change your view of His character?**

____

____

____

____

4. *How have your own plans or expectations limited what you believed God could do in your life?*

5. *How has God used wounds from your past to develop compassion or grace in you?*

6. *In what areas of your life do you find it hardest to trust God's goodness—especially when His timing doesn't match yours? What fears lie beneath that struggle?*

SECTION III

ALIGNING WITH GOD'S TRUTH means allowing His Word to reveal where your patterns drift from His design and your ways have grown comfortable but are not His. It's the brave surrender of choosing His path over your own, trusting that even when it feels stretching or unfamiliar, His ways are carrying you into greater freedom.

14

Crushed by Perfection, Freed by Grace

I stood frozen at the piano, my fingers hovering over the cold keys, unable to play a single note. Not because I didn't know the chords my teacher had shown me, but because the weight of my own expectations had paralyzed me. In that moment of stillness, God whispered a truth that would finally set me free.

> *But God shows and clearly proves His [own] love for us by the fact that while we were still sinners, Christ (the Messiah, the Anointed One) died for us. Therefore, since we are now justified (acquitted, made righteous, and brought into right relationship with God) by Christ's blood, how much more [certain is it that] we shall be saved by Him from the indignation and wrath of God.*
>
> ROMANS 5:8–9 (AMPC)

"What did you do?" My mother's sharp tone pierced deeper than the crystal shards scattered at my feet. Four simple words hung in the air above the shattered crystal—words that would begin to shape decades of my life. Reflecting on that moment years later, I wondered if eleven was really too young to have been entrusted with such fragile treasures.

That morning began with such promise. Sunlight streamed through open windows on that spring Saturday, dancing across the polished surface of our china cabinet. My fingers traced each delicate curve of crystal and porcelain pieces as I lifted them from their sanctuary, each with stories etched in their patterns. I hummed while going through the familiar ritual of cleaning day, occasionally distracted by the dust motes floating in the golden morning light.

Our Saturday ritual flowed like a quiet dance—her gentle washing in the kitchen, my careful drying and carrying each treasure to its place in the dining room. I felt the weight of her trust, positioning each treasure with reverent precision, creating a display that spoke of care and belonging.

Then in one heartbeat, everything changed. My attention wavered for just a moment—distracted by who knows what. Then came the sickening sensation of something precious slipping from my grasp, followed by the explosive sound of shattering crystal against the hardwood floors.

Time froze. The music stopped. My mother's quick footsteps rushed toward the sound, her small frame suddenly in the doorway, her voice making up for what her stature lacked.

I stood paralyzed, surrounded by broken fragments that seemed to mirror my breaking heart. Little did I realize then, in that crystalline moment of failure, perfectionism made its home in my spirit. It became an armor I forged from fear, promising safety, but eventually delivering a heaviness so crushing I often crumbled beneath its unforgiving weight.

For years, perfectionism became my constant companion, hovering like a critical spectator as I stood before unfinished canvases, my brush frozen mid-stroke. Small imperfections grew enormous in my sight until I could no longer see beauty—only an endless inventory of flaws.

Like every child, I had once believed trouble came simply as a consequence of behavior. The equation seemed so simple, good behavior earned praise—mistakes brought punishment. Yet years later as a therapist, I came to a profound realization.

My parents' rigid discipline wasn't just about control. It reflected the deep-seated anxieties they struggled with as immigrants navigating an unfamiliar culture. Their desire to protect us from what they saw as dangers around us created an environment where avoiding mistakes became our priority. Fear of punishment made us walk on eggshells—conversations halted at approaching footsteps, laughter died at disapproving glares. At times, anxiety sat like a brick on my chest, making each breath a conscious effort. My perfect facade concealed a heart overflowing with emotions I couldn't express—slowly suffocating the very person my perfectionism was meant to protect.

Books piled high beside my bed, courses filled my shelves, yet the gnawing certainty that I wasn't quite "enough" eroded any confidence I managed to build. I lived stranded between the person I was and the impossible ideal I believed I should be.

My carefully constructed perfect persona began to unravel during the early years of my marriage, when we settled in a small Florida town and joined a tiny local church. There, I met a friend who saw through my polished exterior with discerning eyes that somehow still reflected God's love. When she spoke truth, her words quenched something parched within me, yet when those same truths pointed to my flaws, my throat tightened, my eyes burning with tears. Though I tried to listen with an open heart, shame overtook me. I often stared at the floor, crumpling inward, unable to bear the weight of my own humanity.

After one particularly difficult conversation with my friend, depression settled over me. As I sat heavy-hearted on the couch, the piano seemed to call me. I rose, drawn to the keys as if by invisible threads. The moment my fingers touched the cold ivory, Proverbs 15:8 came to my mind. *The prayer of the upright is Your delight.*

The word upright stood out to me, compelling me to look deeper. It meant righteous, honest, without fault—someone with pure intentions and integrity. Someone who is good.

Though my heart longed to live rightly, I could only fixate on my failures and flaws. Then, Romans 5:8–9 (AMPC) broke through my darkness like dawn after a long, sleepless night.

> *But God shows and clearly proves His [own] love for us by the fact that while we were still sinners, Christ (the Messiah, the Anointed One) died for us. Therefore, since we are now justified (acquitted, made righteous, and brought into right relationship with God) by Christ's blood, how much more [certain is it that] we shall be saved by Him from the indignation and wrath of God.*

Suddenly, those sacred words loosened chains I hadn't known were binding me. Despite years of walking with Christ, it was then I finally grasped His grace—His acceptance even when my failures outweighed my successes. Healing began unexpectedly when I discovered this liberating truth—God had never placed those demanding standards on my shoulders. He loved me perfectly in my imperfection.

Before this moment, sadness had muffled my prayers into silent, shame-drenched whispers. I couldn't even lift my eyes heavenward. But now God was gently revealing the flaw in my thinking, inviting me to embrace my humanity—my beautiful, broken, imperfect self.

> There's freedom in accepting our limitations while still working to grow beyond them.

The simple truth is, humans make mistakes. Perfection remains forever beyond our grasp, no matter how much we strive for it. And that's okay. There's freedom in accepting our limitations while still working to grow beyond them.

God, in His infinite wisdom, carved a path for us to approach Him despite our imperfections. While we were yet sinners—living in rebellion or oblivious to our shortcomings—He demonstrated His love for us by dying on the cross for us. And because of THAT supreme act of love, we ARE righteous, brought into right relationship with Him through the sacrifice He made for us.

As I sat at the piano that day, the words from Proverbs 15:8 washed over me. I scrambled to capture them.

> *The prayer of the righteous is Your delight.*
> *The prayer of the righteous is Your delight.*
> *It's only Your blood that makes me righteous, Lord!*
> *Therefore, my prayer is Your delight.*

There is nothing any of us can do to become right with God. It is only the blood of Jesus that makes a person righteous. Jesus Christ's sacrifice and the cleansing of His blood allows us, despite our flaws, to stand freely before Him, granting us access to His love and grace. And even more importantly, we can visualize God's delight when we come to converse with Him in prayer. We should not feel bound by the crushing weight of perfectionism any longer. While we remain broken and flawed, we are also perfectly loved—our shattered pieces held in hands that delight in creating beautiful treasures from our fragments.

Heavenly Father,

I come to You with all my broken pieces that reflect my humanity in all its imperfection. For so long, I've carried the weight of trying to be perfect, believing that's what You wanted from me. I thought if I could just be good enough, flawless enough, then maybe I'd earn Your love.

> While we remain broken and flawed, we are also perfectly loved—our shattered pieces held in hands that delight in creating beautiful treasures from our fragments.

But You've been showing me the truth. You don't delight in my perfection. You delight in me. Your love doesn't depend on me getting everything right. It flows freely, even when I mess up.

Forgive me for believing I had to earn Your approval, for thinking Your love was something I could lose if I wasn't perfect enough.

Thank You for the blood of Jesus that makes me righteous—not because of anything I've done, but because of what He's done. Not through my striving, but through His sacrifice.

Help me remember that when You look at me, You see Your child. You see me covered by Christ's righteousness, perfectly loved despite my imperfections. My prayers matter to You not because I've got it all together, but because I'm Yours.

Father, take these broken pieces of my life and make something beautiful from them that reflect Your glory.

I'm letting go of the need to be perfect. I'm embracing the freedom to be human. And I'm resting in this truth: I am broken, flawed, and perfectly loved by You.

In Jesus' name, Amen.

A Moment of Reflection

1. What unspoken rules or expectations from childhood still shape you? How might understanding them help you release perfectionism that no longer serves you?

    ____

    ____

    ____

    ____

2. Was there a moment that planted seeds of perfectionism in your heart? How might revisiting that memory with compassion change how you see yourself today?

    ____

    ____

    ____

    ____

3. Where do you adjust your behavior, lower your voice, change your opinion, or hide your feelings, to avoid disapproval? What would it feel like to stay fully yourself in those moments?

    ____

    ____

4. *How would your prayers change if you truly believed God delights in you regardless of performance? What would you say without shame's filter?*

5. *Do you still struggle with moments that overwhelm you with shame? What thoughts or situations trigger you to "crumple inward"?*

6. *What practice could you begin this week to exchange shame for God's delight? How might you create your own "piano moment"—a space to hear His truth about who you are in Him?*

15

Trading in Burdens for Peace

What if the burden you carry is an invitation to a sacred exchange? We often stagger beneath life's crippling burdens. We worry about loved ones in danger, futures uncertain, financial storms threatening, past regrets haunting quiet moments. Yet in Scripture's ancient wisdom lies a liberating revelation. These weights were never yours to carry. The Creator offers a divine transaction—your suffocating heaviness for His perfect peace—through a sacred act. Cast your burdens onto shoulders that can bear the weight of the world.

Therefore humble yourselves under the mighty hand of God [set aside self-righteous pride], so that He may exalt you [to a place of honor in His service] at the appropriate time, casting all your cares [all your anxieties, all your worries, and all your concerns, once and for all] on

Him, for He cares about you [with deepest affection, and watches over you very carefully].

1 PETER 5:6–7 (AMP)

Have you ever felt so overwhelmed by an emotion or problem that it threatens to consume every corner of your mind? Your chest tightens. Your shoulders hunch forward. Sleep eludes you as thoughts spiral endlessly. Then, as if drawn by some deep instinct, you seek out someone to talk to—someone who listens with their eyes locked on yours, their presence steady and unrushed. Almost miraculously, as words tumble out, met by empathetic ears, something shifts. The burden somehow becomes lighter, no longer threatening to break you. You notice your breathing deepens. The vise grip around your chest loosens. This is the beautiful mystery of shared suffering.

The Creator offers a divine transaction—your suffocating heaviness for His perfect peace—through a sacred act. Cast your burdens onto shoulders that can bear the weight of the world.

On the other side of this sacred exchange, perhaps you've been the one lending that listening ear. How often has someone approached you, their face etched with worry, shoulders bent beneath invisible weight? They rarely seek solutions. No—what the human heart craves in these moments is simply presence. As they empty their troubled thoughts, their tangled feelings, into your waiting silence, you witness the transformation—their expression softens, their posture straightens, as if gravity itself has loosened its hold. What they needed was someone to help shoulder the weight that had become too heavy to bear alone.

This is why the Scripture encourages us in Galatians 6:2 (AMP):

> *Carry one another's burdens and in this way you will fulfill the requirements of the law of Christ [that is, the law of Christian love].*

This truth cuts to the heart of our design—we were never meant to carry our burdens alone. When we do, anxiety whispers like static in our ears, making it impossible to hear the clear frequencies of truth beneath the noise. Our world becomes smaller. Colors fade. Joy retreats. We find ourselves trapped by fear, our view of life narrowing until all we can see are our problems.

But in reaching out—in the vulnerable courage of sharing our struggles and the quiet strength of lending an ear—we find our lifeline. In this sacred exchange lies a seed of hope. Together, we find the strength to rise above challenges that once seemed insurmountable.

Sometimes, however, after holding space for another's pain, you feel it—it's as if their burdens have slipped from their shoulders onto yours. Their worries then seem to echo within you, each concern finding resonance in your own heart. So how do we remain present without becoming unintentional containers for others' heaviness? Especially in the midst of our own life's challenges? 1 Peter 5:7 (AMP) helps us find a balance:

> *Casting all your cares [all your anxieties, all your worries, and all your concerns, once and for all] on Him, for He cares about you [with deepest affection, and watches over you very carefully].*

The word "casting" in the original Greek isn't gentle—it's a violent, deliberate action. It means to hurl, to throw with force, to fling something away from yourself with intention. Picture this, a weary traveler on a dusty road, shoulders bent beneath a pack grown too heavy to bear. With deliberate movement, they fling that burden onto the back of a waiting donkey. The relief is immediate, observable in every loosened muscle.

This powerful word appears only once more in Scripture—in Luke 19:35, where they cast their garments on the colt Jesus would ride into Jerusalem. This parallel reveals God's divine purpose. Just as the disciples flung their garments to prepare the way for Christ's triumphal entry, we too must act with the same deliberate intensity. Muscles straining. Strength failing. We cast—deliberately hurling our burdens onto Him with the force of desperate trust.

Through that act, the crushing weight lifts in an instant. You can breathe again—deep and full. As the tension melts away, this sacred surrender liberates every part of you. You exchange your heavy, suffocating anxieties for His peace. And then—just as Jesus promised, *"For my yoke is easy and my burden is light"* (Matthew 11:30, NIV). What happens in this deliberate transfer is miraculous. Worries that once consumed you fall away, creating space for His peaceful presence to gradually fill every corner of your once-burdened heart.

The word "care" in 1 Peter 5:7 translates as anxiety—representing every hardship, complicated circumstance, or affliction tightening your shoulders and robbing your sleep. It's anything that twists your stomach into knots and sends your mind racing down dark corridors of worst-case scenarios. As worry infiltrates our lives, it works like a silent enemy, gradually undermining our immune system, dismantling our natural defenses with each racing heartbeat, each shallow breath. It steadily carves away at our body's strength until illness finds an easy path into our weakened system. We were not designed to carry burdens, fears, and anxiety. They bend us toward earth when

> We were not designed to carry burdens, fears, and anxiety. They bend us toward earth when we were created to stand tall, faces lifted toward heaven.

we were created to stand tall, faces lifted toward heaven.

The second part of the verse says, *for He cares for you.* Here, "care" means to notice with painful attention—to be meticulously aware of every detail with deep concern. This contrast powerfully illustrates the exchange that happens when we cast our cares on God—showing both what we lose (the weight and depletion) and what we gain (being lifted and replenished). When we come to Him with our burdens, He doesn't glance casually our way. Christ focuses with laser precision on our needs, His attention unwavering.

Isn't it freeing to know that you don't have to carry anything by yourself? Take the challenges you are facing, the things that wake you at 3:00 a.m. with your heart pounding. The heavy concerns for loved ones that make your chest tight. And cast them. Don't set them down gently. Hurl that heavy baggage onto the One who can shoulder it. Picture yourself at the airport check in counter. It's time to surrender your baggage. Let it go. Watch it disappear down the conveyor belt, out of your hands at last.

God isn't distantly interested in your life—He's intimately invested in every detail, every tear, every whispered fear. He cares about what makes your heart race at midnight. He invites you to real conversation, to speak the unspeakable, to give Him what hurts the most, and to sit in the quiet of early morning. Paper and pen in hand.

In the quiet space that opens up after casting your burdens, a gentle dialogue often begins to emerge. Write to God like you'd write to your closest friend. Take time to pause in the silence and listen, noting what rises in your spirit. You might wonder, *How do I know these gentle whispers are His voice and not just my own thoughts?*

The answer rests in how they make you feel. If these quiet impressions bring peace, if they wrap around your heart like a warm blanket on a winter night, if they make you feel truly seen and deeply loved— then know it's Him. No one gives more loving attention to your needs than Jesus, who counts even the hairs on your head and catches every tear you cry in a bottle. The shoulders that carried the weight of a heavy, wooden cross up Calvary's hill for you, are waiting to carry the weight of your burdens today.

> The shoulders that carried the weight of a heavy, wooden cross up Calvary's hill for you, are waiting to carry the weight of your burdens today.

Heavenly Father,

In this moment, I come to You with everything that weighs on my heart. The worries that tighten my chest, the fears that keep me awake at night, the burdens I was never meant to carry alone—I cast them all upon You now.

Forgive me for the times I've clutched these anxieties so tightly, believing the lie that I must handle everything myself. With deliberate trust, I now fling these heavy concerns onto Your capable shoulders, just as Your Word invites me to do.

Lord, thank You for the sacred gift of community—for those who listen with compassion and steady presence. Help me to both receive and offer this beautiful exchange of burden-bearing love. When others share their struggles, give me strength to be fully present without becoming weighed down.

In the quiet space that opens after releasing my cares to You, tune my heart to recognize Your gentle voice. When peace wraps around me like a warm blanket, when I feel truly seen and deeply loved—help me know it's You speaking to my soul.

Thank You that the same shoulders that carried the cross for me stand ready to carry my burdens today. I choose to exchange my heavy anxieties for Your peace that passes understanding.

In Jesus' name, Amen.

A Moment of Reflection

1. *In what areas of your life are you still trying to carry burdens alone? What would it look like to truly "cast" them onto God with the forceful intention described in 1 Peter 5:7?*

____

____

____

____

2. *When was the last time you felt physically lighter after sharing a burden with someone? What prevented you from reaching out sooner?*

____

____

____

____

3. *How has your body been signaling to you that you're carrying weight not meant for your shoulders? (Consider your sleep patterns, tension in your body, breathing, energy levels).*

____

____

____

____

4. *How might your perspective shift if you truly believed that God notices your struggles "with painful attention" and unwavering focus?*

____

____

____

____

5. *In what ways has carrying others' burdens helped you fulfill "the law of Christian love" in your relationships? Where is God calling you to extend this ministry of presence?*

____

____

____

____

6. *What specific burden feels heaviest right now? Visualize yourself at that airport check-in counter—what does it feel like to watch that particular baggage disappear down the conveyor belt?*

____

____

____

16

He Ain't Heavy—
He's My Brother

Have you ever felt the weight of carrying someone else's burdens, their struggles pressing into you, their pain pulling you down? God never intended for compassion to crush us. He shows us how to lift others with grace, how to give without losing ourselves, so their load grows lighter while your strength remains steadfast.

> *For everything we know about God's Word is summed up in a single sentence: Love others as you love yourself.*
>
> GALATIANS 5:14 (MSG)

As a little girl, I would lose myself in the lyrics of *He Ain't Heavy, He's My Brother*, letting my imagination roam. I pictured a long, perilous journey, my younger brother in my arms, shielding him from danger with unwavering determination. I was a skinny nine-year-old girl, barely tipping the scales at seventy pounds, while my 4-year-old brother, restless and full of energy—weighed forty. It was far from realistic, but my fierce love for him defied reason, convincing me I could accomplish the impossible.

Looking back, I wonder what prompted a child to entertain such profound thoughts. Perhaps my own traumas shaped this longing to protect, planting seeds of compassion deep within me. Whatever its origin, this desire to protect and help others grew, eventually influencing everything from my closest relationships to my career choices.

My heart has always been drawn to help those in distress, my heart reaching out, sometimes before my mind has fully processed the situation. Over time, I've recognized this as part of God's intricate design—crafting me with a compassionate heart and an empathetic spirit that connects deeply with the pain others carry. Scripture affirms this calling, particularly in Galatians 6:2 (NIV).

> *Carry each other's burdens, and in this way you will fulfill the law of Christ.*

Yet after decades of ministry, a counseling degree, and multiple certifications, I found myself drained—stripped of joy and struggling to carry my own burdens, let alone someone else's. The flame of passion to save others flickered in the winds of exhaustion, leaving me questioning the very pursuits I once embraced.

As I wrestled with those feelings, I leaned on a foundational truth shaped by years of walking with God. Rather than questioning His Word, I needed to question my interpretation of it. Rather than doubting His nature, I had to reassess my view of Him. Where had things become misaligned?

If I was called to support others, why was I so exhausted? After all, God said that He came to give us not just life, but life in abundance.

John 10:10 (AMP) says:

The thief comes only in order to steal and kill and destroy. I came that they may have and enjoy life, and have it in abundance [to the full, till it overflows].

Seeking further, I read The Message translation of Galatians 5:22. It painted a picture of the Spirit-filled life—exuberance, serenity, compassion—that seemed to exist in a different universe than my depleted reality.

But what happens when we live God's way? He brings gifts into our lives, much the same way that fruit appears in an orchard—things like affection for others, exuberance about life, serenity. We develop a willingness to stick with things, a sense of compassion in the heart, and a conviction that a basic holiness permeates things and people. We find ourselves involved in loyal commitments, not needing to force our way in life, able to marshal and direct our energies wisely.

What was I missing? As I studied and meditated on the Word, one Scripture became very clear to me.

For everything we know about God's Word is summed up in a single sentence: Love others as you love yourself.

GALATIANS 5:14 (MSG)

The spotlight suddenly shifted. I had mastered loving others, but what about loving myself? How was I nurturing and protecting myself? I had never really seen the second part of the equation. The cold realization washed over me—I couldn't remember the last time I'd shown myself the same grace, patience, or care I readily extended to everyone else. For years, I had poured myself out for others without pausing to refill my own cup. It became clear that neglecting self-care would ultimately leave me unable to help anyone else.

The truth was, I couldn't continue this pattern without eventually reaching the point of burnout. I couldn't pour from an empty cup. Conversations with my husband and close friends echoed in my mind—gentle urgings to establish boundaries and honor my limitations. It was time to seek the Lord for clarity on this inner struggle.

Growing up in survival mode meant emotional needs often went unacknowledged. Had my desperate drive to rescue others actually been a disguised cry to be seen and rescued myself? The question hung in my mind, uncomfortable but necessary. Coming to terms with this reality brought a mix of sadness and freedom.

My empathetic nature had become both a gift and a burden— allowing me to sense others' needs while blinding me to my own. Physical exhaustion signaled before emotional recognition could catch up. Ironically, prioritizing my self-care would actually benefit the people I cared most about.

Learning to tune into my own feelings—to notice the tightness in my shoulders before it became pain, to recognize when I was becoming emotionally overwhelmed before it became breakdown— became a daily practice. Setting boundaries no longer felt like selfishness but stewardship. Monitoring stress levels, prioritizing sleep, and engaging in activities that sparked joy weren't luxuries but necessities.

This journey of restoration taught me the missing element, loving others as myself requires

> This journey of restoration taught me the missing element, loving others as myself requires loving myself first.

loving myself first. Not with selfish intent, but with faithful stewardship. To revitalize, reinvigorate, and re-energize ensures I have the strength to help carry the load for those God strategically brings into my life.

The melody of *He Ain't Heavy, He's My Brother* now plays differently in my heart—the fruit of wisdom hard-earned. What God revealed through my exhaustion wasn't failure but invitation to receive before giving, to fill before pouring out. In the quiet moments of self-nurturing, I discovered that boundaries aren't barriers to compassion but the very foundation of sustainable love.

> In the quiet moments of self-nurturing, I discovered that boundaries aren't barriers to compassion but the very foundation of sustainable love.

The sacred rhythm of receiving God's love and extending it outward creates a beautiful harmony that honors both the giver and receiver. Through this divine balance, I've learned to draw from deeper wells than my own limited reserves. My brother isn't heavy when I have become strong enough to carry him.

Father,

You've seen your children carry weights too heavy for our frames—I'm no different. I've often crossed invisible lines—taking on what was never mine to bear while neglecting my own needs.

Give me wisdom to recognize my weariness before it overwhelms me. Show me when to pause. Like Jesus, show me when to withdraw despite the pressing needs around me. Help me honor this sacred rhythm of retreat and renewal.

When my shoulders ache with others' burdens, teach me the courage to rest. Not as selfishness—but as faithful stewardship of what You've entrusted to me.

Whisper truth when guilt tries to speak, reminding me that empty vessels have nothing to pour out.

In those quiet moments of self-care, draw me deeper into Your presence. Fill me completely. Then, when You call me to carry another's burden, I can do it from a place of strength, rather than strain.

In Jesus' Name, Amen.

A Moment of Reflection

1. When you think about self-care, does it feel like a luxury or a necessity? What's behind that feeling?

____

____

____

____

2. How does your body try to get your attention before you're emotionally ready to admit you're depleted? (Consider tension, exhaustion, sleep patterns, physical pain.)

____

____

____

3. Think about the last time you extended grace, patience, or care to someone else. When was the last time you offered that same tenderness to yourself?

____

____

____

4. *The devotional asks: "Had my desperate drive to rescue others actually been a disguised cry to be seen and rescued myself?" Does this question stir anything in you? What might your pattern of helping others be covering up?*

5. *What would it look like to love yourself with the same fierce compassion you extend to others? What specific boundary or practice would that require?*

6. *If you're honest, what are you afraid will happen if you stop pouring yourself out for others and start filling your own cup first?*

17

When Anger Becomes a Messenger

Most of us were taught to suppress this powerful emotion, fearing it makes us ungodly. But what if anger isn't always a villain? What if through introspection we could use it as a tool for awareness and personal growth?

> *Be angry [at sin—at immorality, at injustice, at ungodly behavior], YET DO NOT SIN; do not let your anger [cause you shame, nor allow it to] last until the sun goes down.*
>
> EPHESIANS 4:26 (AMP)

As a child, my life mission was to make my parents happy. I learned to tread carefully, attuned to other people's moods as the stressors in the house mounted. To be honest, it was more for my sake than theirs. My father's stern demeanor—the way his eyebrows would furrow like storm clouds gathering—and his short temper were quite the motivators. The deep thunder of his voice still echoes in my memory. It was as if the walls trembled when he screamed. Too many times, I had watched the consequences unfold when one of my siblings displeased him.

> But what if anger isn't always a villain? What if through introspection we could use it as a tool for awareness and personal growth?

I remember one evening, sitting in the car with my father, the vinyl seats hot and sticky against my legs, parked outside a store, waiting while my mother rushed inside to pick up a few things we needed. It wasn't long before my father's restlessness became evident. First came the sighs. Then the shifting in his seat. Frustration built like a brewing storm, soon erupting into a flurry of complaints about how long she was taking. Soon, I found myself joining in his frustration, mirroring his agitation, my small hands clenching into fists in my lap. But then, an unexpected thought interrupted, shifting my perspective. *What good is this anger? It won't bring her back any faster. Knowing how impatient Dad is, I'm sure Mom is in a state of anxiety, her heart racing as she hurries as fast as she can.*

Even at six years old, a realization clicked into place: *Patience* was a skill worth mastering. I took a breath, long and slow, and let my imagination carry me beyond the stifling atmosphere of the car toward a place of creativity and calmness. I envisioned somewhere far from my father's discontent, far from the heavy hush of waiting. That day, patience didn't just become a concept—it became my steadfast friend, a companion I would call upon throughout my life.

As I grew up, observing the devastating effects of anger on people and relationships, like a wildfire consuming everything in its path—it became a dreaded emotion—one I feared and consciously guarded against with vigilance. Anger became a bad word for me; a foul taste I refused to let linger on my tongue. To me, anger was dangerous, an emotion to be avoided at all costs. Of course, if you asked my little brother, I'm sure he could recount times he saw me get angry. Let's just say it was a bit like the telenovelas—those dramatic Spanish soap operas my grandmother loved—complete with theatrical exits and slammed doors.

Years later, in a conversation with friends, the topic of anger came up. Pat, a wise counselor with eyes that seemed to read my soul, pointed out that anger is simply an emotion, like any other feeling—neither inherently good nor bad. Her words landed like stones in still water, creating ripples of discomfort that were hard for me to swallow. In fact, she treated every emotion as an informant, a detective examining clues at a crime scene.

I resisted the thought. It was hard to accept, until I remembered Matthew 21, Jesus in the Temple, flipping over merchant tables. The image is vivid: coins clinking across the stone floor, doves fluttering to freedom, merchants scrambling to salvage their profits.

Jesus wasn't reckless. He was righteous. His anger wasn't uncontrolled rage, but a response to injustice. He reacted out of anger because the merchants were exploiting people with overpriced goods. Moreover, throughout the Old Testament, God Himself expressed His anger. It wasn't mindless wrath. It was always rooted in love, in justice, in a desire to be heard. In fact, Proverbs 6 states that there are things God actually hates, and provides a list that reads like a divine line drawn in the sand. Proof that anger has a place.

That conversation with Pat sent me on a quest that completely reframed my perspective of the subject. I explored anger not as an enemy, but as a signal. Now, I am no longer fearful of anger or intimidated by this emotion. I no longer see it as a monster lurking in the shadows of my heart. In addition, by recognizing that anger is often a secondary emotion—typically overshadowing another feeling—I now probe deeper. I look beyond my immediate feelings to uncover the underlying emotions anger might be covering.

While I recognize anger's potential dangers, its ability to scorch relationships and leave scars—I've discovered it can also be a tool for self-awareness, offering me valuable insights about myself and others, like a flashlight illuminating dark corners.

It speaks to what lies beneath. When anger flares, instead of taking it at face value, my friend taught me to search for the hidden evidence. There are hurt feelings concealed beneath harsh words, fears disguised as frustration, unmet needs masquerading as irritation. I've learned to pause, to look beyond my immediate feelings to uncover the underlying emotions anger might be covering, like peeling back layers of an onion to reach its core. When I feel anger rising, I learned to ask myself: *What is this really about?*

I've also learned that anger can serve as a guardian emotion, standing at the gates of our hearts, protecting us so our boundaries are not violated. It tells us when we're being taken advantage of, when we're overlooked, when something isn't sitting right. Anger can make us aware of a need that we have, whether they're needs we haven't learned to communicate or physical needs we've ignored.

I've seen it in my grandchildren—meltdowns over minor things when they're tired or hungry, their little minds unable to communicate discomfort any other way. Unfortunately, I have discovered that when I'm tired or "hangry," I also turn into a grumpy version of myself that others would rather not experience.

However, I also understand how destructive anger can be, having experienced its negative impact. For some people, anger has been the only way to express their needs or desires, the only language they know how to speak fluently. The negative consequences of anger— broken relationships, regretted words, shattered trust—highlight the importance of "finding our voice" to communicate in a healthier way, learning to speak with clarity instead of erupting in flames.

Ultimately, anger serves as both a protective signal and a potential obstacle. By moving beyond anger to communicate effectively—trading roars for reasoned words—we nurture healthier relationships and enhance our understanding of ourselves. Transformed into a tool for constructive dialogue, anger no longer controls us—it empowers us. It can then become a tool for personal growth, where we can use constructive dialogue instead of destructive outbursts. As a result we have more fulfilling connections, turning what could be a weapon into a bridge that connects rather than divides.

> By moving beyond anger to communicate effectively—trading roars for reasoned words—we nurture healthier relationships and enhance our understanding of ourselves.

Dear Father,

In moments when anger burns within me like wildfire, quiet my spirit enough to hear Your whisper. Help me see beyond the flames to what lies beneath—the tender hurts, the unspoken fears, the boundaries crossed.

Transform my anger from a weapon that destroys into a light that illuminates truth. When I am tempted to bury my feelings in silence or explode in harmful ways, teach me instead to speak with both courage and compassion. Let my anger be clean, righteous—free from the poison of bitterness, yet honest enough to honor the heart You gave me.

In my relationships, grant me the wisdom to respond rather than react, to seek understanding before judgment. And in those sacred moments when righteous anger rises against injustice, let it fuel not my pride but my purpose in Your Kingdom. For You, Lord, are slow to anger yet perfect in Your justice—may my emotions increasingly reflect Your divine nature. Amen.

A Moment of Reflection

1. *Think of the last time you felt angry. What more vulnerable emotion might have been hiding underneath—fear, hurt, disappointment, feeling unseen or unheard?*

2. *When anger flares in your relationships, does it usually signal an unmet need or a violated boundary? Is there a pattern you notice?*

3. *In what ways has your family's approach to anger shaped how you express or suppress this emotion today? What did you learn about anger being "safe" or "dangerous"?*

4. *The devotional describes anger as both "a protective signal and a potential obstacle." Where in your life right now is suppressing your anger actually causing more harm than expressing it would?*

____

____

____

____

5. *Consider a relationship where unprocessed anger has created distance. What specific truth are you avoiding speaking because you're afraid of how your anger might come out?*

____

____

____

____

6. *If anger is a messenger, what message has yours been trying to deliver that you keep refusing to hear?*

____

____

____

____

18

Teflon® or Velcro®?

That harsh comment from three years ago? You still remember exactly where you were standing when you heard it. But yesterday's genuine compliment? Already gone, like smoke in the wind. It's strange how our minds seem wired to hold onto every sideways glance, every delayed text, every moment that feels off—like we're collecting evidence in a case against ourselves. But what if we could flip the script—become Velcro® for grace and let negativity slide off like Teflon®?

> *Finally, believers, whatever is true, whatever is honorable and worthy of respect, whatever is right and confirmed by God's word, whatever is pure and wholesome, whatever is lovely and brings peace, whatever is admirable and of good repute; if there is any excellence, if there is anything worthy of praise, think continually on these things [center your mind on them, and implant them in your heart].*
>
> PHILIPPIANS 4:8 (AMP)

Philippians 4:8 offers a gentle nudge in that direction. It's not just "think happy thoughts." It's an invitation to center our minds on what's true, lovely, and life-giving. Romans 12:2 reminds us that transformation starts in the mind. It's not instant, but it's possible.

Psychologists like Dr. Rick Hanson describe this perfectly. "The brain is like Velcro for negative experiences, but Teflon for positive ones"—catching every harsh word while letting compliments slip away.[1]

Trauma intensifies this pattern. Children who walk on eggshells around an angry parent develop hyper-awareness to every sigh, every frown, every change in tone. I lived this way for years. A friend's delayed text? My mind immediately went to work. *What did I say wrong? Are they upset?* Instead of asking the vulnerable question, "Hey, are we okay?" I'd build entire stories around imagined slights.

For me, passive-aggressive communication literally rewired my brain. Each eye roll, each silent treatment, each time I had to guess what someone really meant—it trained my mind to become a detection machine. I started scanning every interaction for what could go wrong, replaying critical moments on a loop while positive ones faded into the background. Psychologists call this negativity bias. It doesn't just appear overnight. It's learned, trained, reinforced until it becomes our default setting. Sadly, negativity bias doesn't just affect our thoughts. It takes a toll, straining our relationships.

The Israelites knew this struggle intimately. Picture them, finally free after 400 years of slavery, walking through the wilderness toward promises they could barely imagine. Yet what do we hear from them? Complaints.

---

1 Rick Hanson, "Take in the Good," accessed November 5, 2025, https://www.rickhanson.net/take-in-the-good/. See also Rick Hanson, "Taking In The Good," *Psychology Today*, February 6, 2010, https://www.psychologytoday.com/us/blog/your-wise-brain/201002/taking-in-the-good.

"What are we supposed to drink?" they grumbled to Moses. Not, "God, you've done the impossible before—what's your plan now?" Just complaints. "This water tastes terrible. We're tired of manna. At least in Egypt we had decent food."

Their trauma had trained them to see lack instead of provision, problems instead of possibilities. They had walked on dry ground between walls of water. They had seen Pharaoh's army swallowed by waves. Yet their minds returned to what was missing, what was hard, what wasn't enough.

Generations of being told they were worthless, of every hope crushed, of expecting the worst took its toll on the Israelite people. Even freedom couldn't undo that conditioning overnight. Their negativity bias wasn't a character flaw; it was a survival skill that outlived its usefulness.

I get that. Maybe you do too.

Here's what's heartbreaking about their story, their constant complaints revealed their struggle to trust Moses as their leader and to believe in God as their provider. For 400 years, Pharaoh had been their authority figure—cruel, unpredictable, using them for his own gain. So, when Moses showed up talking about freedom, when God began performing miracles, some of them couldn't help but wonder, *What's the catch? When will this leader turn on us too?*

How often do we interpret God through the lens of an absent father, a critical boss, a disappointing authority figure? Past trauma can rewire our default from trust to suspicion. How often have I allowed past hurt to color present grace? We become prisoners of our own perspective, held captive by a negativity bias that keeps us from seeing God, and others, as they truly are.

The cruel irony? The very mechanism meant to keep us safe begins to steal our joy. We become so good at spotting potential problems that we miss actual blessings. We dismiss compliments as politeness but hold onto criticism as truth. We explain away love but embrace rejection as proof of what we've always suspected about ourselves.

But here's the shift: Philippians 4 isn't asking us to ignore reality. It's inviting us to reframe it. To let truth challenge our automatic thoughts.

Paul reminds us that transformation begins in the mind:

> ***Do not conform to the pattern of this world, but be transformed by the renewing of your mind.***

ROMANS 12:2 (NIV)

And when worry threatens to overwhelm us, pastor and author Eugene Peterson, translator of *The Message*, reminds us of what prayer can do:

> ***Let petitions and praises shape your worries into prayers, letting God know your concerns. Before you know it, a sense of God's wholeness, everything coming together for good, will come and settle you down.***

PHILIPPIANS 4:6–7 (MSG)

God suggests we fill our minds with things that are true, noble, authentic, compelling, gracious—the best, not the worst—the beautiful, not the ugly.

Paul doesn't just say "think positive." He gives us a practical roadmap. Instead of letting worry write the story, he says, "Take it to God first. Say, 'God, I'm reading this as rejection, but what do you see? Help me see this through Your eyes.'"

Then listen. Give God space to challenge your automatic thoughts. This isn't about putting on rose-colored glasses. It's about taking off the dark ones. It's about intentionally creating space for truth, beauty, and goodness to take root. It's about becoming Velcro® for grace.

Sometimes thoughts feel like runaway trains. That's when we need 2 Corinthians 10:5 (NIV).

We take captive every thought to make it obedient to Christ.

You have the power to capture spiraling thoughts before they capture you. Practice looking for and catching the good. Let those true, noble, authentic, compelling, and gracious ideas stick around long enough to take root.

> Practice looking for and catching the good.

Choose to challenge assumptions. Maybe that distant friend is going through something. Maybe that compliment was sincere. Maybe God's silence isn't punishment—it's presence.

This isn't about perfection. It's about practice. Training our minds to look for God's goodness the way we once searched for signs of trouble. Giving others the benefit of the doubt the way we wish they'd give it to us.

God's posture toward you? Always love. Always hope. Always an invitation. He's not passive-aggressive. He doesn't play games. When He's quiet, it's not because He's upset with you.

So, the next time negativity tries to stick like Velcro®, remember: you have a choice. You can let it cling, or you can focus on what is true, lovely, and praiseworthy. You can become Teflon® for negativity and Velcro® for grace.

The Israelites eventually made it to their promised land, but many missed the daily miracles along the way because they were too focused on what was lacking. Don't let that be your story. Your promised land might be closer than you think. You just need new eyes to see it.

Father,

You know my story. Father, help me learn to trust when my instinct is to worry. Help me pause before I panic. When interactions feel uncertain, when I'm tempted to read rejection where none exists—remind me that love is patient, love is kind.

Like the Israelites, help me notice Your goodness, Your provision instead of lack.

I've seen You part seas in my life—and still worried about the next wave. You've provided manna for today, and I've fretted about tomorrow's bread. Forgive me for trusting my fears more than Your faithfulness.

Rewire me, Lord.

When criticism comes, help it slide right off. But when encouragement whispers my name—let it stick. Let it take root. Let it grow into something beautiful.

Help me become as good at spotting Your blessings as I am at spotting problems.

Help me see You as You really are—not through the broken lens of human disappointment, but with eyes washed clean by Your love. You don't play games. You don't withhold affection when You're upset. When You're quiet, it's not punishment—it's presence.

Transform my mind, one thought at a time.

When I spiral into worst-case scenarios, remind me to bring my worries to You first. Give me courage to ask vulnerable questions instead of building bitter assumptions.

Fill my mind with what is true. Noble. Pure. Lovely.

> God's posture toward you? Always love. Always hope. Always an invitation.

Help me become someone who gives others the benefit of the doubt—the same grace I long to receive. When a friend seems distant, give me courage to reach out with compassion instead of retreating in hurt.

My promised land might be closer than I think—I just need new eyes to see it. Help me notice the daily miracles I've been missing while focusing on what's lacking.

Let this be my story, Velcro® for Your grace, Teflon® for the enemy's lies.

In Jesus' name, Amen.

A Moment to Reflect

1. *Think about a harsh comment or criticism from your past that still lives in your mind. Now think about a genuine compliment from around the same time. Which one do you remember more clearly? Why?*

____

____

____

____

2. *Like the Israelites in the wilderness, what "miracles" in your current situation are you overlooking because you're focused on what's missing or difficult?*

____

____

____

____

3. *When someone's text is delayed or their tone feels off, where does your mind go first? What story do you automatically tell yourself?*

____

____

____

____

4. *Think about a relationship where you often assume the worst. What is that negativity bias costing you in that connection?*

____

____

____

____

5. *If you could rewire one automatic thought pattern that's keeping you stuck, what would it be?*

____

____

____

____

6. *When God is silent in your life, what do you assume about His feelings toward you? Where did you first learn to interpret silence that way?*

____

____

____

____

19

When Molehills Become Mountains

Have you ever watched your mind take a small worry and turn it into an epic disaster movie? We've all been there—caught in a downward spiral of worst-case scenarios, losing sight of reality. But what if there was a way to catch yourself before you tumble all the way down that rabbit hole? What if the solution was simpler than you think?

> *He replied, "I have been very zealous for the LORD GOD Almighty. The Israelites have rejected your covenant, torn down your altars, and put your prophets to death with the sword. I am the only one left, and now they are trying to kill me too."*
>
> I KINGS 19:14 (NIV)

"We will never find it! It's lost forever! I'll never be able to play with my drone again."

Watching a child react and lose it over a lost toy can feel heartbreaking and amusing at the same time. One minute they're laughing, the next they're sobbing like their world has ended. As adults, we shake our heads and think we've outgrown such dramatic reactions. But have we really?

The truth is, parts of us remain stuck in childlike patterns, surfacing when we least expect them. For those familiar with anxiety, it can feel like an unstoppable train, racing toward hopelessness with no exits in sight. There's actually a name for this mental spiral: *catastrophizing*.

You know that feeling when your brain decides to become a Hollywood director, crafting elaborate disaster plots with you as the helpless victim? That's catastrophizing in action—when our minds take a real situation and blow it up into something much bigger and scarier than it actually is. Worst-case scenarios become so vivid that our bodies react as if they're already happening—heart racing, palms sweating, drowning in imagined doom.

It's like a runaway freight train. You catch a friend's eye at church and offer a smile—but get no response. Did she miss it? Or did she choose to look away? The thought lingers, growing heavier. Was it something I said last week? Did I offend her? By the time service ends, the weight of silence has transformed into certainty. *She doesn't like me anymore.* This kind of thinking doesn't just steal our peace—it invites the very anxiety and hopelessness we're trying to avoid.

This isn't a struggle new to man. Even biblical heroes wrestled with distorted perspectives, unable to see past their fears.

Take the Israelites, for instance. Fresh from witnessing God part the Red Sea, they spotted Pharaoh's army in the distance and immediately jumped to the worst conclusion.

"Was it because there were no graves in Egypt that you brought us to the desert to die?"

EXODUS 14:11 (NIV)

But perhaps no one illustrates this better than Elijah. Elijah sat beneath the brittle branches, the heat of the wilderness pressing against his weary frame. He wasn't just running—he was unraveling. His calling felt hollow, his faith weakened. Fear whispered, *You are alone.* And for a moment, he believed it. Elijah's despair didn't just distort his situation—it clouded his sense of who he was and what God had called him to do.

Here was a man who had just witnessed God send fire from heaven, defeating 450 prophets of Baal in a dramatic showdown. You'd think he'd be riding high on faith. Instead, one threat from Queen Jezebel sent him spiraling into such despair that he ran for his life, collapsed under a tree, and declared himself the last faithful person on earth.

But here's where the story gets beautiful.

God didn't respond with a theological lecture about faith or a scolding about dramatic thinking. Instead, He did something wonderfully practical. He let Elijah sleep. Then He fed him. Twice. Because sometimes our catastrophic thoughts are really just our soul's way of crying out for basic care—rest, nourishment, and connection.

Then came the gentle correction. Paraphrasing, 1 Kings 19:18, God said, "Actually, Elijah, there are 7,000 others who haven't bowed to Baal." Notice the magnitude of the number. Seven thousand. Not seven, not seventy, but seven *thousand* faithful people that Elijah's exhausted mind had somehow overlooked.

Usually a result of trauma, catastrophizing often happens when we are tired, overwhelmed, and overpowered with fear. It's our mind's misguided attempt to protect us by preparing for every possible disaster. But instead of preparing us, it overcompensates and paralyzes us.

Recognizing our vulnerability is crucial. When we've poured out everything—spiritually, emotionally, physically—we become like phones with low batteries, prone to glitching and shutting down unexpectedly. By taking proactive steps to restore our energy through rest and nourishment, we can guard against exaggerating our circumstances and magnifying the negatives.

But here's another key insight from Elijah's story: Isolation amplifies catastrophizing. When we're alone with our thoughts, molehills morph into mountains with alarming speed. That's why avoiding isolation and instead connecting with supportive companions who can lift us up and remind us of God's unwavering promises isn't just helpful, it's essential. These connections prevent fear from taking over and stabilize us in our faith.

> Avoiding isolation and instead connecting with supportive companions who can lift us up and remind us of God's unwavering promises isn't just helpful, it's essential.

Shortly after this reality check, God introduced Elijah to Elisha—a companion who walked with him for the rest of his earthly journey. And here's the remarkable thing. There's no record of Elijah ever experiencing that same depth of despair again. Connection, it turns out, is catastrophizing's greatest enemy.

> *Also, if two lie down together, they will keep warm. But how can one keep warm alone?*

ECCLESIASTES 4:11 (NIV)

The wisdom in these ancient words rings just as true today. When we're isolated in our thoughts, everything feels colder, harder, more impossible. But connection brings warmth—not just emotional warmth, but the kind of clarity that melts away our frozen fears.

The next time your mind pulls you onto the runaway train of worst-case scenarios, think about Elijah under the tree and his weary, distorted perspective. Let it remind you that your perception isn't always reality—and that God's view of your situation is far more accurate, and far more hopeful, than your own. You're not alone, even when it feels like you are.

And remember too: your greatest breakthrough may be just one divine connection away.

God never intended for us to walk through the challenges of life alone. He knows how easily we turn molehills into mountains. That's why He doesn't just offer us truth—He offers us a community of support to help us see clearly when our vision gets clouded by fear. The next time your mind starts spinning anxious scripts, remember: God is writing a different story altogether.

Father,

When I carry unnecessary weight, when my fears are magnified, and my worries spiral—remind me of Your truth.

Remind me that You are not a God of confusion or fear. You are the God of peace, the anchor in the storm. You are steady when my thoughts feel scattered, and You remind me that fear does not have the final say.

Lord, when I feel unsettled, when my thoughts run wild and anxiety tries to grip my heart, help me to pause before I believe the worst. When doubt whispers that I am alone, remind me that You are near, working even in ways I cannot see. Replace my restlessness with Your presence, my despair with Your hope.

Speak truth into the places where doubt has settled. Replace despair with the assurance that You are working even in the moments I cannot understand.

Teach me to rest in You—to trust that my feelings do not define reality. Give me wisdom to discern the voice of fear from the voice of faith. And when I find myself unraveling, let Your love be the thread that holds me together.

I surrender my catastrophizing and my need for control. I choose instead to believe You are present and that You are faithful.

In Jesus' name, Amen.

A Moment of Reflection

1. What worry has your mind recently turned into an "epic disaster movie"? When you take away the movie, what's the actual situation?

____

____

____

____

2. When you're catastrophizing, what does your inner voice sound like? Does it remind you of someone's voice from your past?

____

____

____

____

3. Think of a specific time when you were convinced something terrible was going to happen, but it didn't. What can you learn from that gap between your fear and reality?

____

____

____

4. *Like Elijah isolated under the tree, where in your life are you trying to carry something alone that's making your fears grow bigger?*

____

____

____

____

5. *Take a moment to ask God to speak to you about your situation. What insight does He want you to have regarding it?*

____

____

____

____

6. *If you stepped back from the catastrophic thoughts, what might you see differently about your situation?*

____

____

____

____

20

Oil and Water: The Duck's Secret to Resilience

Have you ever watched water bead up and roll off a duck's feathers? The bird remains dry while surrounded by water. What if our hearts could do the same with offense? What if hurtful words and misunderstandings could touch our surface but never penetrate our peace? Resilience isn't just surviving life's challenges—it's emerging intact from them.

> *It is not rude; it is not self-seeking; it is not provoked [nor overly sensitive and easily angered]; it does not take into account a wrong endured.*
>
> I CORINTHIANS 13:5 (AMP)

"You need to be more resilient," my friend said matter-of-factly. "You know, like water off a duck's back."

The words stung for a moment. My cheeks warmed with embarrassment at not understanding what seemed like such a common expression. Silence followed as I searched my friend's face for clues, trying to hide my complete confusion. Ducks? Water? What did waterfowl have to do with anything we were talking about?

The metaphor might as well have been spoken in another language. Our friendship had deepened; our conversations had grown more transparent. But as someone trained to read between the lines and search for hidden meanings in casual remarks, my old habit had an adverse effect. I became the world's worst translator of conversations that didn't need translating in the first place.

At the time, I didn't understand what she was talking about, but I knew my friend was observing something in me that needed to shift. She was right. Some truths hit you like a splash of cold water, startling at first but ultimately refreshing. They unsettle us only to restore us.

The day my friend challenged me about resilience I clutched her words tight and carried them home. They weighed heavy. Truth often does.

That night, I researched ducks and discovered something fascinating. They have a special gland that produces oil, which they spread over their feathers during grooming. This natural practice helps the ducks keep their feathers healthy. God's creation often carries the most profound life lessons, doesn't it? Hidden in plain sight, waiting for us to discover them.

As I sat in my quiet space, Bible open on my lap, I whispered a simple prayer. "Lord, grow resilience in me."

Searching for wisdom, I found it. Psalm 119:165 (KJV) jumped from the page, words illuminated as if highlighted just for me.

> *Great peace have they which love thy law: and nothing shall offend them.*

The verse echoed in my mind. *Nothing shall offend them.* Nothing. My heart raced. Could I get there? Freedom from offense seemed as miraculous to me then as a duck staying dry in a downpour. I hungered for more understanding, flipping pages with growing excitement until Colossians revealed more wisdom.

So, chosen by God for this new life of love, dress in the wardrobe God picked out for you: compassion, kindness, humility, quiet strength, discipline. Be even-tempered, content with second place, quick to forgive an offense. Forgive as quickly and completely as the Master forgave you. And regardless of what else you put on, wear love. It's your basic, all-purpose garment. Never be without it.

COLOSSIANS 3:12–14 (MSG)

I closed my eyes. The image of a duck—its feathers beaded with water that simply rolled away, flashed in my mind. The duck doesn't fight the water; It simply carries within itself the oil that forms a barrier between threat and harm.

"What do I need to do to become more resilient?" I whispered to the Holy Spirit.

The picture became clearer. Oil. Water. Washing. A paraphrased version of Ephesians 5:26 surfaced in my memory. *We are cleansed by the washing of water with the Word.*

And Psalm 133:1 (NASB1995) declares, *Behold, how good and how pleasant it is For brothers to dwell together in unity!*

My clenched jaw relaxed as revelation washed over me. The tension I'd carried, that constant readiness to protect myself, finally released its grip. I saw how God delights in unity and that taking offenses breeds division. Every time I took offense, invisible walls went up. Division grew. Unity crumbled. God wasn't just teaching me about personal peace, He was revealing how my sensitivity affected every relationship in my life.

John Bevere explains in *The Bait of Satan* that offense is a trap Satan uses to pull believers into captivity and hinder their freedom.[1] Reading it, I suddenly saw the hook hidden in the bait for the first time. The enemy doesn't show up with horns and a pitchfork. He arrives with an invitation to be righteously offended.

This lesson didn't transform me overnight. Far from it. My newfound resilience resembled a fragile seedling at first—easily uprooted by harsh words or perceived slights. Opportunities to practice surfaced weekly. Sometimes daily. Honestly? Sometimes hourly. The world serves up chances to take offense as regularly as vegetables at mealtime.

But like any muscle, resilience strengthens with use. Each time I chose not to take offense, something shifted. The water rolled off a little easier. My capacity to love as described in 1 Corinthians 13:5 expanded. I was not easily offended and kept no record of wrongs.

> When misunderstandings arise, pause. Breathe. Consider the offense an invitation to grow stronger, not a reason to retreat.

Opportunities to be offended still present themselves daily. Some days, the stinging water threatens to soak through to my skin. But as for me—I choose love.

In every relationship, offenses will come. They're inevitable. But resilience determines whether they become defining moments or passing events.

---

1 John Bevere, *The Bait of Satan: Living Free from the Deadly Trap of Offense* (Charisma House), theme summarized from published discussions of the book.

When misunderstandings arise, pause. Breathe. Consider the offense an invitation to grow stronger, not a reason to retreat.

What does true resilience look like in practice? It grows from three essential qualities: empathy to understand others' perspectives, patience to respond rather than react, and honest communication that builds bridges instead of walls.

Resilient people don't avoid difficult conversations—they transform them into opportunities for deeper connection that don't just resolve, but restore. They don't simply seek solutions, but search for healing.

It's allowing difficult truths to refine you rather than define you. Each conflict navigated with grace builds a bridge. Each grace extended creates a stronger bond. "Water off a duck's back" isn't about pretending the rain doesn't fall. True resilience doesn't deny the downpour—it rises above it. It's standing in the rain, unshaken, because you've been equipped with the oil of grace and the armor of love.

> Resilient people don't avoid difficult conversations—they transform them into opportunities for deeper connection that don't just resolve, but restore.

Conflict, when met with compassion, becomes a bridge. Grace, when extended, becomes a bond. Resilient love doesn't retreat—it restores. And when love leads, even the hardest conversations become holy ground.

Father God,

Thank You for creating such wisdom in Your world. Even in a simple duck, You've placed lessons that can transform our hearts.

> When love leads, even the hardest conversations become holy ground.

Forgive me for the times I've clung to offense as if it were my right. When hurtful words have pierced me, when misunderstandings have built walls.

Pour Your holy oil over my spirit today. Let it seep into every wounded place, every sensitive corner of my heart that reacts too quickly to perceived slights. Prepare me for the inevitable waters of offense that come with loving imperfect people in an imperfect world.

Remind me to pause. To seek Your perspective before I respond.

Lord, make me like Colossians describes, compassionate, kind, humble, even-tempered, and quick to forgive. Help me wear love as my basic, all-purpose garment, never leaving home without it.

Make me brave enough to have difficult conversations with restoration as my goal.

May each bridge I build through navigated conflict honor You. May each bond strengthened by extended grace reflect Your nature. And may the water roll off my back—not because I'm pretending it isn't raining, but because You've equipped me with everything I need to stay spiritually dry in life's storms.

In the name of Jesus, Amen.

A Moment of Reflection

1. In what ways might you be misinterpreting others' words or actions by "reading between the lines" rather than taking them at face value?

____

____

____

____

2. How has your family background shaped your tendency to either take offense quickly or let things roll off your back?

____

____

____

____

3. Which relationships in your life currently need the oil of resilience to restore connections damaged by misunderstandings or hurts?

____

____

____

____

4. *Are there specific people or situations that consistently trigger you? What does that reveal?*

____

____

____

____

5. *Think of a recent conflict. Were you trying to win or restore? What might shift if you chose restoration?*

____

____

____

____

6. *Are you currently holding onto an offense that God is inviting you to release? What's making it difficult to let go?*

____

____

____

____

21

Deeply Rooted and Securely Grounded

The invisible roots beneath a mighty oak tell more of its strength than its towering branches ever could. Similarly, what grounds our relationships often remain unseen yet determines whether they will weather life's fiercest storms or topple at the first strong wind. God crafted our hearts for more than having simple bonds with others—He designed them as gardens where love transforms us from the inside out.

May He grant you out of the riches of His glory, to be strengthened and spiritually energized with power through His Spirit in your inner self, [indwelling your innermost being and personality], so that Christ may dwell in your hearts through your faith. And may you, having been [deeply] rooted and [securely] grounded in love, be fully capable of comprehending with all the

> *saints (God's people) the width and length and height and depth of His love [fully experiencing that amazing, endless love].*
>
> EPHESIANS 3:16–18 (AMP)

"Love is all we need." Right? Wrong! Whoever said that clearly never had to compromise on thermostat settings in a marriage.

In those early days, we clung to each other, floating on cloud nine—blissfully unaware that our emotional baggage hadn't been left at the altar. My husband arrived with a front-row ticket to his parents' surprise divorce drama, while I brought my own case study in family tension, courtesy of immigrant parents who turned simple conversations into verbal wrestling matches. We were starry-eyed and certain we'd written a different script for ourselves.

Dreams bloomed. Possibilities seemed endless. Yet the shadows were already there, waiting.

As time passed, our past traumas collided like mismatched puzzle pieces being forced together. We were still deeply in love, but our different backgrounds created an invisible wall between us.

"I can't handle this anymore," I hissed through clenched teeth, the words sharp as broken glass. We were in the bedroom—our designated battlefield—where smiles and cheerfulness could be abandoned behind a closed door. I held back the scream I wanted to release. Each clipped syllable landed like hammer strikes, not meant to wound, but to somehow pierce the wall between us and draw out what my heart so desperately needed to express.

My husband stood with his back against the dresser, spine rigid, chin slightly raised. Defense mode. His body language read like a fortress—standing up straight, defiant—silently challenging me to bend first.

Somewhere in the house, our children had likely retreated to their rooms, turning up music or burying themselves in books to escape the tension. Our voices, despite our best efforts, were never as muffled as we wanted them to be. The thought made my stomach twist with a familiar guilt.

We had vowed never to bring up the "D" word (divorce) or hurl insults at one another, but even with these guardrails in place, our arguments still felt dangerous, like driving too fast on a mountain road. If only our pastor had handed us communication tools along with those wedding rings. Instead of vague advice about "never going to bed angry," we needed someone to decode the mystery of why his silence felt like abandonment to me and my questions sounded like an interrogation to him.

We were like two travelers with different maps of the same territory, constantly bewildered by the other's wrong turns. When he retreated into the quiet sanctuary of his thoughts, I mistook his silence for coldness. When I needed to process feelings aloud, he experienced my words as an overwhelming flood.

We'd never seen healthy conflict modeled—just his parents' polite avoidance that ended in a sudden divorce, and my parents' unfiltered verbal sparring. We were trying to build something neither of us had blueprints for. Some nights we'd lie awake in bed, backs turned, each wondering if love was supposed to be this hard. The distance between our bodies measured in inches, but it felt like miles.

Altered by years of hurt, it became a ritual—one of us always walking out, the door slam, a punctuation mark ending conversations too painful to finish. Hours, sometimes days of silence stretched between us. We were both lost, unsure where to start a conversation.

"I'm sorry," we finally learned to say—two simple words that cost our pride everything but gave our marriage a chance. We learned to "care-front" instead of confront—to speak truth wrapped in gentleness rather than wielding honesty like a weapon. To stop the runaway train of our arguments, recognizing the moment when eyes glazed over and hearts closed off.

I did everything I could to heal my heart, break old patterns, and help him put down his defenses. It meant showing patience when every fiber of my being wanted immediate resolution. It meant offering love when my instinct was to withdraw it to protect myself. It meant trying to understand this man from Venus when I'd spent a lifetime on Mars, speaking an entirely different emotional language.

But what we had was too precious to surrender. Sometimes we didn't even know how to come back, what words could possibly repair the damage. So, we just awkwardly returned to shared spaces, cautiously rebuilding the bridge that had collapsed between us.

My husband and I have worked hard to dismantle the defenses that created barriers between us. Years later, our relationship has blossomed into something I couldn't have imagined during those battlefield days. I watch him now across our kitchen, catching the morning light as he reads, occasionally looking up to share something that made him smile. Our laughter comes easily now, rising and falling like a well-practiced duet. The vulnerability that once terrified us has become our sanctuary—a safe harbor where masks and armor have no place.

Through countless conversations and moments of shared transparency through the years, we learned to speak with more than words—our hearts began to talk.

My father's emotional distance—which was probably less about me and much more due to the crushing stress he lived under to provide—became the template I unknowingly laid over my husband's actions decades later. A silent dinner, a missed glance, a distracted nod, all transformed by my unhealed pain into deliberate rejection.

But reality tells a different story than emotional lies. That night when my husband barely spoke? He was worried about layoffs at work. The day he snapped at my question? His neck pain had reached a level eight, but he'd said nothing. He was actually trying to protect me, not wanting to worry me. None of it was about me—all of it was battles he carried silently.

We tend to be more patient with a hungry child when they snap at us than with an adult who does the same. We understand the child's behavior isn't personal—it's about their unmet needs. What if we stopped and considered that the same might be true of the adults in our lives? What if, instead of assuming their actions are a deliberate slight against us, we recognized they might be carrying burdens we know nothing about?

I have always said, "Relationships are God's greatest tools for transformation." One of the most profound lessons God has taught me is the importance of not taking offense quickly at the actions of those close to me. I've learned to pause before reacting, to breathe, and to ask myself about the heart of the person that I know so well. Taking a step back, I consider the bigger picture, asking myself what might really be happening beneath the surface.

> "Relationships are God's greatest tools for transformation."

When I stop jumping to conclusions about someone's motives and instead pause to extend grace, something miraculous happens— the walls between hearts begin to crumble. I've seen stern faces soften, defensive postures relax, and guarded eyes fill with tears of relief at being truly seen, not just judged for their momentary failings. The bridge of understanding I've learned to build with my husband has become the blueprint for every relationship in my life.

I've come to realize that this practice isn't just good relationship advice—it's at the very heart of how God relates to us throughout Scripture. When I read the Bible now, familiar stories reveal deeper truths about God's patience and understanding.

Consider Jonah—not just a reluctant prophet, but a man whose prejudice against Nineveh ran so deep he would rather drown than offer them redemption. What if God had taken Jonah's rejection personally? What if God had matched Jonah's defiance with equal stubbornness? But instead, God pursued him into the depths, offering second chances from inside the belly of grace itself.

Or David—whose passionate heart led him from worshipful Psalms to adulterous betrayal. In the silent aftermath of his sin with Bathsheba, God didn't just write him off. Even though there were consequences, God still saw the heart of the man who had danced before the Ark with unrestrained joy. God sent Nathan not to crush David, but to awaken him from his self-deception—to call him back to himself.

And I can't help but think of that beach in Galilee, where Peter—still haunted by the rooster's crow and his three denials—stood dripping wet at the shoreline. There was Jesus, tending a charcoal fire just like the one Peter had warmed his hands by when he first betrayed the Lord. The smell of fish and smoke must have triggered Peter's shame, but Jesus didn't mention his failure. Instead, three times—matching Peter's three denials—Jesus asked, "Do you love me?" giving Peter the chance not to erase his failure, but to rise above it.

The weight of guilt that had bent Peter's shoulders since that terrible night lifted with each affirmation of love. With each response, his voice got stronger, his eyes finally daring to meet the gaze of the One he had denied. But what he found wasn't condemnation—it was a calling. "Feed my sheep."

Peter's failure didn't mark the end of his story. It was the beginning of his understanding of grace. The God of grace takes the shattered remnants of our mistakes and re-creates them into something beautiful.

Isn't this the heart of the Father in the prodigal son story? While religious leaders muttered about sinners, Jesus painted a portrait of a father scanning the horizon daily, refusing to believe his son was lost forever. And when that distant figure finally appeared on the road—thin, broken, rehearsing his speech of unworthiness, the father hiked up his robes and ran. Dignity forgotten. Appearances abandoned. Arms open wide. Tears streaming. Not a word about squandered inheritance or shameful living. Only celebration that what was lost had been found.

These aren't just ancient tales. They're mirrors reflecting how God sees us—beyond our moments of failure, beyond our patterns of withdrawal, beyond our defenses and disguises—to the beloved heart underneath it all. When this realization takes root, everything changes.

Suddenly, the traffic jam becomes not an obstacle but an opportunity for unexpected reflection. The difficult colleague becomes not an adversary but a soul carrying hidden burdens. The unexpected diagnosis becomes not a punishment but an invitation to discover strength we never knew we possessed. Through this new lens, conflicts become classrooms and misunderstandings melt into opportunities to extend the same grace that has been so freely given to us.

Prayer transforms from anxious petition to intimate communion. I find myself less interested in what God's hands can give me and more drawn to simply resting at His feet, delighting in His presence. My focus shifts from what I lack to what I already possess—counting small mercies that once went unnoticed, morning light filtering through my window, my grandchild's unexpected hug, the perfect sweetness of a summer watermelon.

Being deeply rooted in this love, securely grounded in this grace, creates an unshakable foundation no storm can destroy. It doesn't mean the winds won't blow or the rain won't fall—but it means we won't be uprooted by life's inevitable challenges. From this place of security, joy isn't dependent on perfect circumstances but flows from perfect love. And peace isn't the absence of problems but the presence of Someone greater.

This is the transformative power of being deeply rooted and securely grounded in love—God's love first, which teaches us how to truly love ourselves and each other.

> Peace isn't the absence of problems but the presence of Someone greater.

Lord,

Forgive me for the times I've mistaken silence for rejection, for hearing accusation in questions born of concern, for building walls when You've called me to build bridges.

Like Jonah in the depths, like David in his failure, Like Peter standing ashamed by the shoreline, I have known what it means to fall short. Yet in these very places, You met me with grace beyond measure.

May I be an extension of that same grace. Not taking offense but extending understanding, not demanding perfection but celebrating progress, not holding grudges but offering second chances.

Root me so deeply in Your love, Lord, that my heart becomes a safe harbor for vulnerability, where masks and armor have no place, where laughter rises easily and tears fall freely.

Transform my battlefields into gardens, my misunderstandings into classrooms, my conflicts into opportunities for deeper connection. Let my relationships become living testimonies of Your redemptive work.

And in the spaces where words fail me, where I don't know how to cross the divides I've created, remind me of the Father who runs toward His prodigal children, arms open wide, celebrating what was lost being found.

May I be deeply rooted and securely grounded, not in perfect circumstances but in perfect love, finding my unshakable foundation in You alone.

In Jesus' name, Amen.

A Moment of Reflection

1. *What invisible burdens might the difficult people in your life be carrying that would help explain their actions if you could see beneath the surface?*

______

2. *In moments of conflict, what's your default response—silence, flooding with words, withdrawal, or something else?*

______

3. *Where did you learn that pattern? What filters from your past are you unknowingly placing over present-day interactions with those you love?*

______

4. *Think about a recent conflict where you felt hurt or defensive. What story did you tell yourself about the other person's motives? How certain are you that story is true?*

____

____

____

____

5. *Which is harder for you—offering forgiveness to others or forgiving yourself? What does that reveal about where you're rooted?*

____

____

____

____

6. *What defenses are you still holding onto that keep you from being fully known and deeply loved—by God and by others?*

____

____

____

____

SECTION IV

RECLAIMING GOD'S DESIGN means recovering what was lost or hidden—what was silenced along the way. It's the awakening to who you were meant to be, and the rediscovery of the gifts and purpose life's journey may have buried.

22

Fifteen Seconds to Wonder

The most profound spiritual encounters rarely announce themselves with thunder; instead, they arrive disguised as ordinary moments—a neighborhood walk, a shared laugh, a cooling breeze—waiting for someone attentive enough to recognize their holiness.

> *You will make known to me the path of life;*
> *In Your presence is fullness of joy;*
> *In Your right hand there are pleasures forever.*
>
> PSALM 16:11 (NASB)

Work had been a whirlwind of working through lists, checking boxes, leaving us with a satisfying sense of accomplishment. As we neared my friend Sharon's house, she turned to me with a smile that reached her eyes, "What do you think about taking a walk around the neighborhood, to unwind and talk about our day?" Her voice sounded calm and inviting.

Florida's summer days can be blistering hot, but as dusk starts to fall the heat begins to loosen its grip, shifting the air in our coastal town. It's as if the ocean exhales, sending a cool, refreshing breeze that wraps around us—the day's final embrace before evening settles in like a prayer.

Although the idea was enticing, the spontaneity of it all

> The most profound spiritual encounters rarely announce themselves with thunder; instead, they arrive disguised as ordinary moments

left me unprepared. In true best-friend fashion, Sharon rummaged through her drawers and closet, pulling out a comfy t-shirt for me to borrow, workout pants, and a pair of tennis shoes. My friend's genuine hospitality felt like a warm hug, refreshing and welcoming. Finally, we set out, each step in sync with our commitment to healthy routines. With the day's accomplishments still fresh on our minds, our walk felt like the perfect conclusion to a day well spent.

Within just a few strides, the cool summer breeze caressed our faces. Tall palm trees swayed overhead, their fronds rustling in the breeze. The melodic songs of birds filled the air around us. Without saying a word, we both closed our eyes at the exact same moment, then burst into laughter when we realized what we'd done. Years of friendship had created this unspoken rhythm between us.

I had been studying and teaching at church about the value of savoring, and this moment felt like a divine appointment—a perfect opportunity to pause and practice. As if reading my thoughts, my friend remarked, "It takes fifteen seconds to truly savor a moment."

As we intentionally paused, counting silently and taking in those precious fifteen seconds, a deep sense of gratitude welled up within me.

> "It takes fifteen seconds to truly savor a moment."

It was one of those rare, beautiful moments when everything in life feels right. My workday had been good—productive time with a team I genuinely loved. And now I was ending the day with a dear friend, sharing deep conversation, healing laughter, and the kind of companionship that feels like home. In that heartfelt connection, I felt profoundly grateful, knowing I was experiencing something sacred and fleeting. What more could one possibly ask for when heaven touches earth this way?

Sometimes God makes His presence known in the simplest ways—a gentle wind, a quiet moment, an unexpected peace. It's in times like these that we can experience the wonder of His creation and the comfort of His companionship. When we slow down enough to savor what's right in front of us, we begin to see the sacred in the ordinary.

I wonder, how often do we let the wind pass by without recognizing what a blessing it truly is? How often do we miss moments like this because we're rushing to the next thing, failing to notice God's presence? How often do we take for granted the gift of having someone close that we can openly talk to about the things on our mind—realizing it's a gift not everyone shares?

Today, intentionally take a moment to savor. Tune in to what you see, what you hear, and what you feel—God's fingerprints are everywhere if we'll notice. Take in the beauty of your surroundings with eyes wide open to wonder. Embrace moments of companionship with a grateful heart. We often take these simple moments for granted, forgetting there's no guarantee they'll come again. Each moment is a unique gift—unwrap it slowly.

Father,

I pause now to notice the blessings surrounding me. Help me savor Your gifts rather than rush past them. When life feels full of challenges and difficulties, remind me of the countless blessings You give me every moment.

Thank You for the simple gift of wind on my face and the breath in my lungs. Thank You for reminding me, with every breath, that You're here with me. Help me pay attention today to what I so easily miss—the beauty around me, the friend sitting beside me, the sacred hiding in the ordinary.

Teach me to slow down and really see Your blessings, whether it's the sky at sunset or the smile of someone I love. Help me notice the moments You've given me instead of rushing past them. Open my eyes to see You in the everyday, and give me a heart that's quick to be grateful.

In Jesus' name, Amen.

A Moment of Reflection

1. What are the small moments in your daily life that bring you joy, but often go unnoticed?

____

____

____

____

2. When was the last time you paused long enough to recognize God's presence in an ordinary moment? What did you notice?

____

____

____

____

3. Where might God be inviting you today to take fifteen seconds and notice His fingerprints in your life?

____

____

____

____

4. *Think of a friendship or relationship that feels like "home." How does recognizing it as God's gift change how you receive it?*

____

____

____

____

5. *How often do you rush past the simple blessings God offers—like wind on your face, laughter with a friend, or a moment of peace?*

____

____

____

____

6. *What makes it hard for you to slow down and savor God's goodness in the everyday?*

____

____

____

____

23

Learning to Pause

Sometimes our bodies know what our minds haven't figured out yet—that we're running on fumes and desperately need to hit pause. In our hyperconnected world where productivity is king, the simple act of stopping can feel revolutionary. What if the answer to being constantly overwhelmed isn't what we think it is?

> *Yet the news about him spread all the more, so that crowds of people came to hear him and to be healed of their sicknesses. But Jesus often withdrew to lonely places and prayed.*
>
> LUKE 5:15–16 (NIV)

"Where did you go?" my friend asked, looking back to find me frozen at the restaurant entrance, staring at the menu like a deer in headlights.

One afternoon, after an intense meeting and a deep conversation, we had decided to grab lunch at Panera. I had been there before, but that day it felt overwhelming. The lunch hour crowd made me think of a bunch of crazy ants running in different directions, each toward a different destination.

My friend, confident and decisive, had walked with purpose directly up to the counter to place her order. But when she turned around, there I was—my feet seemingly glued to the ground, my eyes wide open, frozen in place. After hours of handling challenges and significant output, my mind needed a moment to catch up before I made one more decision.

But to understand how I got to that frozen moment, I need to take you back to the beginning.

As a young woman, I lived like I was running a race against time. I'd run into the house, mentally rehearsing my next three tasks before I closed the door. At one point, when my business partner and I were trying to squeeze one more task into a five-minute window, our new friend exclaimed without hesitation, "I don't know how you can fit so much into five minutes." We must've looked like hummingbirds on espresso.

Looking back, I realize I inherited my need for speed honestly. My mother, a woman from Colombia's unhurried, cafe-and-conversation culture, where time moves like honey, suddenly dropped into the Northeast rat race. She juggled two jobs and young children while barely speaking the language. Every morning started a race she was already losing before her feet hit the floor. In those early years, she was exhausted. Period.

And then there was the early morning battle cry. "Where's my keys? Has anybody seen my keys?"

Our morning ritual wasn't family devotions. It was the hunt for lost keys. It was as routine as brushing our teeth. Instantly, all of us dropped whatever we were doing—cereal bowls abandoned, shoelaces half-tied—and scattered like detectives at a crime scene. Under the cushions. Behind the bookbags. In yesterday's coat pockets. We'd race against the clock, knowing that finding those keys was the difference between Mami being on time or starting her day late.

Here's the thing, I learned to be anxious without realizing there was a calm. The constant adrenaline rush felt normal, like background music you don't notice until it stops. I thought the constant adrenaline rush was supposed to be my tasteful cup of coffee—until one day, the coffee turned bitter.

And when that coffee turned bitter, I could taste it. This inherited chaos showed up everywhere in my life. You know that stomach-dropping moment when the receptionist looks up and says, "Ma'am, your appointment was yesterday?"

That was my life—a series of wrong places and wrong times. But nowhere was this more obvious than during our Sunday morning routine.

The Sunday chaos became our family's weekly performance. I'd be on my hands and knees under the bed, hunting for my missing shoe while my husband became my human alarm clock.

"We leave in twenty minutes."

"Found it!" I'd emerge triumphant, hair wild, mascara half-applied, while my toddler wandered by wearing only one sock.

"Fifteen minutes now."

I'd frantically search for matching earrings while stuffing snacks into the diaper bag and looking for shoes that actually fit my three-year-old.

"Ten minutes."

Still searching for that second earring. My five-year-old was nowhere to be found.

"Five minutes."

I applied lipstick while hopping into my own shoes and calling, "Kids! Get in the car!"

"We should have left ten minutes ago." My husband's voice carried that barely-controlled frustration he'd perfected over years of being my countdown timer.

"Just need to find . . . kids, where are your shoes? Why don't you have shoes on?"

"I'll be waiting in the car." The front door would close with that particular thud that said everything.

I'd stand there for a moment, breathless, surrounded by the tornado of my morning, wondering: *Why can't I just get my act together and be on time like most people?*

Then came smartphones—digital taskmasters that promised to make life easier but instead turned every moment into an opportunity for productivity. They turned me into a multi-tasking monster. I found myself checking texts while brushing my teeth, scheduling meetings on the phone while driving, then forgetting to put it in my calendar. I'd celebrate crossing something off my list only to scribble down three more tasks.

I was drowning in my own perceived efficiency—or lack of it. I thought I was being efficient, but the reality is that multitasking is an illusion. Studies show it can actually make us up to 40% less productive, not more.[1] My frantic pace had become a whirlwind that left me anxious, exhausted, and ultimately disappointed in myself.

Eventually, my body began to rebel. Running behind made me constantly irritated. I felt my jaw clench when traffic lights took longer than thirty seconds to change, and I collapsed into bed each night feeling like I'd been emptied out and wrung dry. One evening, staring at my phone through heavy eyes, I whispered to myself, "This isn't living—it's just surviving."

---

1 Joshua S. Rubinstein, Jeffrey E. Evans, and David E. Meyer, "Multitasking: Switching Costs," American Psychological Association, accessed November 4, 2025, https://www.apa.org/research/action/multitask.

It was time to tune into my needs and make deliberate changes to how I managed my schedule.

Turns out I wasn't losing my mind—I was just living in a culture that has lost its way. Researchers have a name for what we're all doing, "chronic busyness" and "performative busyness"—being busy just to appear valuable. Think about it: when someone asks how you are, what do you say? "I'm so busy!" Like it's a badge of honor.

We've glorified busyness, wearing it like it proves our worth. We've turned overwhelm into a humble brag, and made motion into our drug of choice—chasing productivity while starving for peace. But here's the reality. All that rushing around isn't getting us anywhere meaningful. My body figured that out before my brain did, which is how I ended up frozen at Panera.

Standing there, overwhelmed and exhausted, Jesus' words suddenly made perfect sense.

"Come to me, all you who are weary and burdened, and I will give you rest."

MATTHEW 11:28 (NIV)

It was there, standing wide-eyed at the entrance, that I finally understood the value of transitional pauses. A transitional pause isn't complicated—it's a deliberate pause between the scenes of your day where you hit the reset button. Instead of racing from one thing to the next, we stop, we breathe, and check in with ourselves and God. It's a space to gather our scattered thoughts, figure out what we actually need, and make sure we're not leaving pieces of ourselves behind as we rush to the next thing. It's about making sure your soul catches up with your schedule.

Have you ever left a place with a feeling that you have forgotten something? You probably would have benefited from a transitional pause. These pauses help us realize that feeling scattered isn't normal—it's optional. That day I learned that constantly rushing isn't productivity—it's panic in disguise. Although the rush of adrenaline that hustling provides can feel satisfying, the mind and body often are silently crying out for a moment to "catch our breath."

That day with my friend, it only took a couple of minutes for me to stand at a distance from the counter, look at the menu, and gather my thoughts, before I was able to place the order. Those few minutes where I took a pause provided me with exactly what I needed to do the next thing. Transition has now become a part of my everyday lifestyle.

The concept of utilizing transitional moments became crucial when I began my career as a therapist. After spending hours absorbing other people's pain—listening to stories of betrayal, loss, and fear—I'd drive home with their voices still echoing in my head, the day's weight on my shoulders. "I don't know what to do," one client would whisper, while another's angry words about their ex-spouse looped endlessly in my mind.

I learned to carve out an hour when I got home, lying on my comfortable bed with the blinds drawn, letting the familiar scent of lavender anchor me back to myself. Slowly, those borrowed emotions would begin to untangle from my own. The knot between my shoulder blades, where I seemed to carry everyone's burdens, gradually softened. Taking my cares to the Father with each intentional breath, the tension from my body gently disappeared, replaced by a lightness that reminded me who I was beneath all that I carried. This wasn't just rest; it was remembering where I ended and others began.

In this hour of solitude spent with the Holy Spirit, the clutter of the day disappeared, replaced by a calm clarity. After a day of empathetic listening and problem-solving with other people, my heart and mind needed the peace only God could offer me. When I emerged from this quiet place, my spirit was revived, and I was ready to connect. This simple act of transitional stillness replenished me and filled my cup with the capacity to nurture and cherish the relationships waiting for me at home. Instead of giving from a place of depletion, I was able to give from a place of stability and strength.

Jesus often took moments away to recover and reset. Even amidst the commotion around him, the needs of others for healing, and the cries for his attention, Jesus made time for solitude and quiet time. Although He was full of compassion for the needs of the people, Jesus understood the importance of withdrawing from the crowds to anchor Himself in His relationship with God. We see an example of this in our focal passage, Luke 5:15–16.

Jesus prioritized His spiritual needs and lived a life led by the Spirit of God, rather than solely moving to meet the needs of others. Jesus made His decisions about where and when to be somewhere, under the direction of His Father. If Jesus Himself needed these transitional pauses to replenish and hear from God, how much more can we benefit from following His example?

The next time you feel that familiar tug to rush from one thing to the next, remember that even Jesus—who could have healed the whole world in a day—chose to step away and breathe. Your pause isn't procrastination; it's preparation. It's not laziness, it's wisdom. In a world addicted to motion and a culture that glorifies busyness, rest isn't giving up—it's refusing to burn out. It's actually self-care and spiritual obedience. So go ahead—hit pause. Your soul is waiting for you there.

> Remember that even Jesus—who could have healed the whole world in a day—chose to step away and breathe.

Father,

I'm beginning to understand that maybe the way I've been living isn't working. That constant motion doesn't always mean progress. That feeling scattered might not be "normal life."

Help me notice when I need to pause. Not because I'm weak, but because I'm human. Show me that taking time to breathe and check in with You isn't wasted time—it's what keeps me connected to what really matters.

Thank You for Jesus, who showed me it's okay to step away. Even when people needed Him, even when there was more work to do, He found time to be alone with You. Help me follow His example.

Give me permission to hit pause when I need it. To stand at the restaurant counter for an extra moment. To sit in the car before going inside. To take those breaths that help my soul catch up.

When I do pause, meet me there. Help me remember who I am beneath all the roles I play and tasks I carry. Fill me with Your peace so I can move forward from a place of rest, not rushed anxiety.

Thank You that You love me in my stillness and in my motion. Help me find the rhythm You have for each of us.

In Jesus' name, Amen.

In a world addicted to motion and a culture that glorifies busyness, rest isn't giving up—it's refusing to burn out.

A Moment of Reflection

1. *When you think about your typical day, where do you feel most rushed or scattered? What is your body trying to tell you in those moments?*

____

____

____

____

2. *What does being "busy" mean to you? Is it something you wear as a badge of honor, or does it feel more like a burden you can't put down?*

____

____

____

____

3. *Think about the last time you felt frozen or overwhelmed by a simple decision. What had you been doing before that moment? What was your mind and body asking for?*

____

____

4. *How has constant motion become a way of avoiding something deeper in your life? What might you be running from by refusing to pause?*

5. *What inherited patterns of anxiety or busyness have you absorbed without even realizing it?*

6. *Jesus withdrew to lonely places even when crowds needed Him. What is it costing you right now not to follow His example?*

24

Uncrumpled: Restoring the Masterpiece Within

It sneaks in when you least expect it, distorting your perception, twisting reflection into doubt. What brought you joy in the past, now seems insignificant. It can strip the color from your passions, turning confidence into hesitation and creativity into doubt, suffocating potential. What if instead of comparing your gift to someone else's you embraced it? It's time to find freedom from the weight of comparison, so you can embrace what God has given YOU, without reservation.

> *But each one must carefully scrutinize his own work [examining his actions, attitudes, and behavior], and then he can have the personal satisfaction and inner joy of doing something commendable without comparing himself to another. For every person will have to bear [with*

> *patience] his own burden [of faults and shortcomings for which he alone is responsible].*
>
> GALATIANS 6:4–5 (AMP)

"Look at this extraordinary detail in David's painting." Mrs. Thompson's voice dropped to a reverent whisper, her finger hovering just above the paper.

Mrs. Chen leaned closer, eyes widening. "The way he's captured light reflecting off the water, and he's only five. Some children are just born with a gift, aren't they?"

Although they were speaking with low voices, I heard every word, and they cut straight to my heart.

That moment in kindergarten became a turning point—one of those small experiences that leave permanent marks. Like many artists throughout history, my first brush with comparison became a defining moment.

As a little girl, art quickly became my absolute favorite subject. Drawing, coloring, painting, these weren't just activities, they were doorways. Each blank page invited me to step through into a world where my imagination ruled. One memorable morning in Kindergarten, I disappeared into the picture I was painting.

My eyes were wide with excitement as my little fingers moved with purpose. Each brushstroke brought to life what I saw in my mind. I was lost—gloriously, completely lost—in my creation. The classroom faded away. The other children vanished. It was just me and my masterpiece, evolving stroke by stroke. Every now and then I stopped. A feeling of fulfillment rose up in me as I admired the piece before me.

Suddenly, I was jolted back to reality.

A sudden commotion at the table across from mine broke the quiet—hushed voices tinged with excitement. The way the teachers huddled over someone else's desk was like treasure hunters who'd found gold.

For a moment, I dared to hope. Maybe they just hadn't seen mine yet.

I stretched my neck to glimpse what had captured their attention. My classmate's picture lay before them—stunning. Truly a work of art. My eyes darted back to my own painting, searching for that same magic.

But something had shifted. A moment ago, my painting felt brilliant. But now somehow, the colors had dimmed. With lead in my chest, I stared at what moments before had been my masterpiece. Now, it was just paper with paint. Nothing special.

I swallowed hard. My fingers, so confident before, now curled into a tight fist around my creation. Crumple. Toss.

That day, I didn't just discard my artwork—I discarded a dream. A piece of who I was meant to be. The joy I had found in painting was buried beneath the weight of feeling "not good enough."

After that, I rarely picked up a pencil to let my imagination roam freely again.

Comparison has a way of doing that. It doesn't simply whisper criticism—it rewrites your perception. It turns masterpieces into mediocrity, passion into hesitation. What was once full of potential can feel like a mistake. It slips through the cracks of our most vulnerable moments and begins its silent pillaging. Scripture warns us of this trap.

> *But each one must carefully scrutinize his own work . . .*
> *without comparing himself to another.*

GALATIANS 6:4 (AMP)

We've all felt it. The Instagram scroll that leaves us feeling like we don't measure up. The promotion announced for someone else. The ministry that blossoms while ours struggles for root.

Left unchecked, comparison can breed pride, insecurity, and resentment. It becomes a thief—robbing us of joy, stealing the gifts God placed inside us, sabotaging pieces of our destiny. It sneaks in, making you believe your journey is somehow less valuable, simply because it looks different from someone else's.

I wonder how many masterpieces lie crumpled in waste bins around the world. How many books are unwritten? Songs unsung? Dreams abandoned?

But here's the truth: we often compare our raw beginnings to someone else's refined skills. It's an unfair comparison—measuring your first chapter against their entire book, crafted through thousands of hours of practice.

God calls us to grow our gifts, not compare them. He isn't measuring perfection—He's searching for faithfulness. Our unsteady attempts matter more to Him than another's polished performance. What He treasures isn't the flawlessness of your creation, but the love with which you create. Your canvas isn't in a competition; it's cradled in the hands of a Father who smiles at every stroke.

> God calls us to grow our gifts, not compare them. He isn't measuring perfection—He's searching for faithfulness.

Your gift matters. Not because it's better than anyone else's. Simply because it's yours.

Today, I invite you to name the comparison thief. Where has it stolen from you? What joy has it pickpocketed? What confidence has it lifted?

Then imagine placing your gift—that beautiful, imperfect, utterly unique expression—into cupped palms. Not to measure or weigh against another's, but to offer back to the One who crafted it, He who created you.

Let your gifts unfold in their own rhythm, their own colors, their own time. And watch what happens when you give yourself the freedom to create without comparison. Joy returns, and the masterpiece is restored, while you walk freely into all that God has called you to create. Freedom doesn't come from being the best—it comes from offering your best, and knowing it's enough because it's yours.

> Freedom doesn't come from being the best—it comes from offering your best, and knowing it's enough because it's yours.

Father,

Forgive me for the times I've allowed comparison to become a thief in my life. You've seen every time I've crumpled up a gift You've given me because it didn't feel good enough. You've watched as I've set aside dreams, closed doors on passions, and hidden parts of myself away—all because I measured myself against others, instead of seeing myself through Your eyes.

Today, I want to receive back what comparison has stolen. I'm asking You to restore the joy of creating without fear. Help me to see the specific gifts You've woven into who I am.

When I begin to compare, turn my eyes back to You. Remind me that You delight not in perfection, but in faithfulness. You celebrate not just the masterpiece, but the heart behind it.

Give me courage to create again. To write words that might fumble, to sing notes that might be off key—knowing you are not looking for perfection, but you treasure obedience.

And Lord, help me be someone who celebrates others' gifts without diminishing my own. Let me be a voice that calls out the masterpieces hiding in crumpled hearts around me.

In the name of the One who made each of us a unique reflection of Your creativity, Amen.

A Moment of Reflection

1. *What gifts or dreams have you crumpled up and tossed away because they didn't feel "good enough" compared to someone else's?*

____

____

____

____

2. *Think back to a specific moment when comparison stole your joy. What were you creating or pursuing before that moment shifted everything?*

____

____

____

____

3. *Where in your life today are you most vulnerable to the comparison thief? (Your appearance? Your work? Your parenting? Your creative pursuits? Your spiritual journey?)*

____

____

____

4. *What are you still measuring against someone else's polished performance instead of recognizing as your own beginning chapter?*

5. *If you're honest, what has staying stuck in comparison protected you from? What does it allow you to avoid attempting or risking?*

6. *The devotional asks: "How many masterpieces lie crumpled in waste bins?" What specific masterpiece—what book, song, dream, or calling—is God asking you to uncrumple and offer back to Him today?*

25

Coffee Grounds and Masterpieces: Rescuing What's Yours

The most devastating losses aren't what others take from us. They're what we surrender without realizing it. Doubt whispers. Insecurity nods. And slowly, quietly, we step away from the very gifts God designed us to use, until one day we look up and realize we've walked away from our purpose entirely.

"For to everyone who has [and values his blessings and gifts from God, and has used them wisely], more will be given, and [he will be richly supplied so that] he will have an abundance; but from the one who does not have [because he has ignored or disregarded his blessings and gifts from God], even what he does have will be taken

> *away. And throw out the worthless servant into the outer darkness; in that place [of grief and torment] there will be weeping [over sorrow and pain] and grinding of teeth [over distress and anger]."*

MATTHEW 25:29–30 (AMP)

"You threw it away?" My voice trembled as I stared at the trash can, disbelief crashing over me. This time it wasn't me that had thrown away my picture. The vibrant painting—the one I had painstakingly created—was crumpled amid coffee grounds and torn envelopes. In that moment, something more than my artwork was discarded. A part of me—my passion, my confidence—had been thrown out, too.

This time, it wasn't my own doubt that threw it away—it was my mother, simply focused on cleaning, moving through the house with purpose. She didn't see the hours I had poured into it, the satisfaction that had warmed my heart as I brought color to life on paper. How could she have known this was already my battleground? It touched a bruise that already existed, pressing on a place where the enemy had been whispering lies about my worth, my gifts.

This wasn't the first time my art had met this fate. When I was five, my small fingers had been the ones to crumple my own creation—after comparing it to a classmate's masterpiece, the one that had captivated our teachers' attention. They had marveled at his talent with wide eyes and enthusiastic praise, and in my young mind, their silence about mine screamed that I wasn't enough. So, I crumpled it up and threw it in the trash, deciding I wasn't an artist after all. But one day I would learn that walking away from a gift God has placed within you isn't just hesitation—it's relinquishing a part of the calling He intended for you to fulfill.

However, my father hadn't just noticed the drawings I brought home—he had seen *me*, the artist within. Whenever I sketched, whenever my hands shaped color into form, he would say, *"Mamita, you are like your grandfather. He painted beautiful paintings. You are an artist like him."*

Something in my chest tightened—an unfamiliar mixture of pride and longing. My father's words settled in my heart like an anchor, tethering me to a legacy. I had never known my grandfather, only heard scattered stories about him. Yet, in that moment, my father's words built a bridge between us, spanning across time—his belief in me became my quiet connection to a man I had always wished I had met.

Comparison and insecurity are silent thieves, stealing dreams in broad daylight.

When I was 13, my family moved to Florida at the end of October, delayed by the sale of our previous home. Missing the beginning of the school year meant I began my final year of middle school as an outsider, a stranger in hallways already thick with formed friendships and established routines. Because of the delay, there were just a few elective choices available for my classes, and as God would have it, art was one of them.

At that time, I figured it might be fun to try my hand at art again, to see if the spark still lived somewhere inside me.

My art teacher was a thin woman with long black hair and reading glasses that perpetually slid down her nose. Her passionate discussions about art often left me puzzled. She didn't just *talk* about art—she *felt* it, like it was a spiritual experience. She'd stare at a painting, tilt her head dramatically, inhale as if the colors themselves carried an aroma, and whisper things like, "Look at the emotion in those brushstrokes. Do you feel the movement? The story hidden beneath the layers?" she'd exclaim, her voice breaking slightly as her fingers traced the air above a painting. "Can't you feel the artist's soul speaking to you?" Her eyes would glisten as if she were witnessing something sacred, while my teenaged-self struggled not to roll my eyes.

I'd squint, hoping to catch even a glimpse of what she was seeing, but all I could make out were colors on paper. If there *was* movement, it must have been running too fast for me to catch. She could find depth in a flat canvas, uncover heartbreak in a splash of blue, and interpret the deep agony of a crooked line. Meanwhile, I was wondering if the classroom's fluorescent lighting was messing with my perception.

Honestly, she saw more in art than I could see even if I examined it with a magnifying glass. It was as if she had access to a secret dimension—one where brushstrokes whispered their life stories and colors had emotional breakdowns. I admired her passion, but to me, it felt like she was speaking a language I'd never learned. Perhaps I found it humorous because my heart no longer resonated with art as hers did—the connection had been severed long ago beside a kindergarten trash can.

However, during class one afternoon, I was fascinated by a piece depicting a Mexican man riding a mule. What captivated me most was the serape draped over the man's shoulders, a handwoven blanket that celebrated life through color. Dazzling stripes in hot pink, turquoise, sunny yellow, and royal purple radiated across his frame, each hue more vibrant than the last, as if competing for attention yet somehow creating perfect harmony. The artist had somehow captured both the weaving patterns and the cultural pride embodied in those threads. The serape wasn't just clothing—it was joy made visible; tradition transformed into wearable art. I decided to experiment a bit by painting on black construction paper, hoping the colors would stand out even more vibrantly against the dark backdrop.

Leaning closer, nose nearly touching the print, questions formed. *What made these colors feel so alive? How had the artist made such bold, almost defiant brightness feel so natural, so truthful?*

As I painted this picture, something unexpected happened. Time dissolved around me. The classroom chatter faded to background noise as my brush moved across the paper with purpose. I was engrossed in the process—truly present in a way I hadn't been since kindergarten.

After dedicating several hours over a week, my piece was finally complete. Standing back, I felt something I hadn't in years—genuine pride in my creation. In my eyes, it was truly exceptional. My teacher noticed too, pausing behind me longer than usual, her hand resting lightly on my shoulder as she nodded with a pleased smile that acknowledged my focused dedication.

That afternoon, I brought my art home, the paper still slightly damp, holding it carefully to avoid smudges. I was eager to show my parents, anticipating their reaction with excitement. My father validated my work, as he repeated those words that always warmed me from the inside. I was artistic like his father, who had been a painter.

But a few days later, my heart froze mid-beat. I discovered my painting discarded in the garbage. With desperation, I reached down and grabbed it, brushing off the dry coffee grounds and torn envelopes. Then, relief surged through me. It was mostly unharmed. The colors remained bright. The paper was unmarked, untouched by its surroundings. But then, my breath caught. One edge—just one—had been torn, jaggedly ripped, mirroring the tear in my heart.

I pulled my artwork closer, gripping it as though holding onto more than paint and paper. I was rescuing more than a drawing—I was rescuing *myself*, the part of me that had been cast aside, the part that was struggling to survive.

But gifts don't fade; they wait. And sometimes, it takes someone else to remind us they're worth reclaiming.

After I got married, my husband noticed something settled in me every time I walked around in an art store. It was as if I had finally arrived where I was meant to be—like coming home. I never had to say it out loud. But he saw it. The desire was there, thick in the air, wrapped up in the scent of turpentine and unspoken dreams, hanging between the aisles like an invitation I wasn't yet ready to accept.

I'd trail my fingers along the rows of neatly stacked brushes, pausing to flip through a Bob Ross art book, the familiar scent of oil paints and fresh canvas wrapped around me, stirring something deep within. I had a quiet longing to explore different art mediums—to experience them all. Oil painting, acrylics, pastels. Each one held a unique kind of magic, drawing me in with its possibilities. I found myself mesmerized by paintings, studying every brushstroke, wondering if I had it in me to create something just as beautiful—if I dared to try.

"You should take an art class," my husband said as he saw me staring at the newspaper advertisement. I finally gave in, and on the first day, sat nervously before an empty canvas, paintbrush gripped too tightly in my sweating hand.

Despite enjoying the classes, the swirl of colors, and being with other like-minded creatives, I struggled. I spent more time being hyper-critical of my work than celebrating the experience. I obsessed over every flaw. "Look at how uneven my lines are," I'd whisper to my husband later, pointing out flaws invisible to anyone but me.

"See how the perspective is off here? And this color is all wrong," I'd say, dismissing his praise and minimizing my efforts. Instead of embracing growth, I fixated on imperfection. Everything I made felt disappointing through the distorted lens of my own perception. The soil of his encouragement couldn't take root in the rocky ground of my self-doubt.

One afternoon, a friend dropped by unexpectedly, my large sketchbook open to a drawing illustrating a Scripture with a mountain scene, the verse written above it. Her eyes widened as she stared in disbelief. "Did you do this?" she asked amazed, her fingers tracing the pencil lines with reverence. "I didn't know you could draw like this!" You would think she had just discovered a hidden treasure.

"It's not that great," I mumbled, looking down. "The perspective is all wrong on the mountains."

She just kept staring at the drawing, shaking her head while I kept pointing out everything wrong with it. It was like I couldn't help myself. Someone would complement my art, and I'd immediately tell them why it wasn't any good.

But God wasn't silent. He sends us messengers—voices to remind us, voices of encouragement who see the gifts we reject. He sends them to remind us of the gift we are so reluctant to claim. They call them out, awakening them within us.

God was speaking—through my husband, through friends and family—who saw it when I couldn't. They encouraged, nudged, urged me forward, refusing to let my doubt bury what God had given me. Still, I had to be willing to listen.

Even though I earned a degree in Graphic Design, satisfaction in my creative pursuits remained elusive, like trying to grasp water. It only came during a challenging time in my life, when I embraced photography in my 50s. Looking back at decades of abandoned sketchbooks and half-finished projects, I wish I had spent more time nurturing the creative side of me. Sadly, comparison and insecurity cast long shadows over my gift for many years, robbing me of joy that could have been mine all along.

In retrospect, I have come to realize that God designs us all with unique gifts, attracting us to certain passions for a divine reason.

What we are drawn to often aligns with our purpose. There's intention behind the things that make our heart race and our minds lose track of time. We find true fulfillment as we explore and nurture these gifts. They light up parts of us nothing else can reach. These passions become an integral part of our "God assignment."

The enemy doesn't fear your talent; he fears your obedience to develop it. For that very reason, it is not uncommon for these areas to be targeted by the enemy. Satan aims to disrupt and often even sabotage our divine mission, not through dramatic confrontation, but through the whispered lies of inadequacy and the slow erosion of confidence.

He sends us messengers—voices to remind us, voices of encouragement who see the gifts we reject. He sends them to remind us of the gift we are so reluctant to claim.

God highlighted Matthew 25:14–20, also known as The Parable of the Talents, for me. Reading it offered insights that restored my interest in embracing creativity once more. Matthew 25:29 (AMP) says:

> *"For to everyone who has [and values his blessings and gifts from God, and has used them wisely], more will be given, and [he will be richly supplied so that] he will have an abundance; but from the one who does not have [because he has ignored or disregarded his blessings and gifts from God], even what he does have will be taken away."*

Reading the parable Jesus told illuminated my understanding—there are varying levels of talent, like instruments in an orchestra, each playing a unique but essential part. The violinist doesn't abandon her violin because she can't produce the resonant depth of the cello, nor does the flutist silence his melody because it doesn't thunder like the timpani. Each contributes according to their design.

> What we are drawn to often aligns with our purpose.

Yet how often we silence our own gifts because someone else's seems more impressive. Standing before paintings in galleries, I'd return home with thoughts like: *Why bother? I'll never create like that.* What I failed to see was that my artistic voice—though perhaps quieter or in a different key—had its own audience waiting to hear it.

The truth is, we aren't called to match someone else's brilliance but to fully develop the talent entrusted specifically to us. We each receive different measures of natural abilities or gifts in different areas. Some people might naturally have more artistic talent (like the five talents in the parable), while others might have less (like two talents)—but both are valuable and meant to be developed. The Master's pleasure comes not from the quantity we begin with, but our faithful stewardship of whatever we've been given.

I've also noticed a heartbreaking pattern. Those unwilling to embrace their gifts with discipline, invest in their growth, and risk sharing them with the world often become the harshest critics of others who do. Their envy curdles into bitterness. They become spectators to others' creative endeavors while their own canvas remains blank—not because they lack ability, but because they've disqualified themselves through comparison.

Growth demands both courage and humility. Whether you're learning to paint, to sing, or to speak publicly, there will be moments of vulnerability and uncertainty. When I finally stepped back into art classes, my fingers trembled around brushes held too tightly.

Learning from others more skilled wasn't easy—pride and insecurity fought for control. But what if the masterpiece God imagined through you remains unfinished because you couldn't bear the vulnerability of making mistakes? Because you felt embarrassed when your beginner efforts looked basic next to others with years of practice?

Investing in your gifts is a deeply personal and empowering journey.

Being patient with yourself in this process is key. *Masterpieces aren't painted in a day.*

God sees beauty in your unsteady efforts. He treasures your investment in whatever gift He gave you—whether artistic, relational, professional, or ministerial. Your flawed, imperfect creations, with all its mistakes, is the sacred studio where He shapes your character while you shape your craft. Perhaps it isn't so much about what you create, but about who you become while creating it.

As you continue developing your gifts, the gap between vision and ability narrows, but only if you're brave enough to cross the bridge of imperfection first. Undeveloped gifts can't fulfill their purpose. The five-talent servant didn't wake up to doubled investments. He worked while others slept, practiced while others played, persisted while others quit.

Your gifts, whatever they may be, whisper of divine fingerprints. They carry echoes of God's voice saying, "This one, this talent—I reserved for you alone." No one else can contribute your specific melody to the world's symphony. The potential God placed within you stays dormant until you have the courage to awaken it.

Time invested in your God-given abilities isn't wasted. It's sacred. Each hour spent developing what makes your heart come alive isn't just self-improvement, it's worship. Your willingness to step out in your giftings, despite fear, honors the Creator who designed you to reflect His image. And sometimes, the simple act of showing up faithfully to the work He's given you unlocks doors to possibilities you never imagined.

The greatest regret isn't failure. It's letting fear silence the dream before it ever has a chance to live.

The world needs your courage to become all God created you to be. It needs what only your unique combination of gifts, experiences, and perspective can offer.

What if the greater act of worship isn't perfection, but participation? What if your willingness to steward what He's entrusted to you—however imperfectly—brings more joy to the heart of God than you've ever imagined? Don't let comparison steal what God intended as a blessing. The gift He placed within you isn't just for you. It's for a world waiting to experience His creativity through the miracle of your willing hands and heart.

Today, pick up what you've discarded. Reclaim what was stolen. Your Father is watching, and He delights in seeing His children create.

Dear Father,

Today I come to You with hands once empty, holding fragments of dreams I once discarded. Forgive me for burying what You planted, for dismissing my gifts because they didn't meet my expectations.

You grieved as I crumpled my creation, You saw value in my efforts when I saw only flaws. The gifts You wove into my being weren't mistakes—they were invitations to partner with You.

Lord, I confess my fear of imperfection, my reluctance to be a beginner—my hiding behind comparison. Forgive me for the years I let comparison steal, for believing the lie that my offerings fell short. Thank You for those You sent to uncover what I buried, for their eyes that saw value when mine could not.

Give me courage to pick up what was stolen, to embrace the sacred journey of growth. To work while others sleep, to persist when I want to quit. Help me to find joy in the process, not just the product.

Help me remember that when I create, I reflect You, the Creator. May my willingness bring You joy, even when my hands tremble with doubt.

Today, I reclaim what the enemy tried to take. I choose stewardship over fear. Faithfulness over perfection. Worship through the work of my hands.

For when I create from this place of surrender, it's not about what I can or cannot do—it's about allowing Your Spirit to move through willing hands.

In Jesus' name, Amen.

A Moment of Reflection

1. *What activity causes you to lose track of time? What makes your heart come alive when you engage in it?*

2. *What God-given talent or passion have you set aside because of comparison, criticism, or self-doubt?*

3. *Can you identify a specific moment when the joy in this gift was stolen? What happened, and how did it change you?*

4. *Has God sent someone into your life to call out gifts you've been reluctant to claim? How have you responded to their encouragement?*

____

____

____

5. *When you imagine fully developing this gift, taking classes, practicing publicly, risking imperfection—what fear rises up in you?*

____

____

____

6. *The devotional warns: "The greatest regret isn't failure. It's letting fear silence the dream before it ever has a chance to live." What dream is God asking you to pick up out of the trash today?*

____

____

____

26

When Dreams Find Their Rest

Sometimes the most profound revelations come wrapped in the simplest questions. A casual conversation at my front door became a moment of shifting mindset—when I discovered that chasing dreams and finding peace aren't opposites, but dance partners. What if contentment isn't about settling for less, but about recognizing where you need to be present for now? This is the story of how I learned to breathe in the space between ambition and gratitude.

Not that I speak from [any personal] need, for I have learned to be content [and self-sufficient through Christ, satisfied to the point where I am not disturbed or uneasy] regardless of my circumstances. I know how to get along and live humbly [in difficult times], and I also know how to enjoy abundance and live in prosperity. In any and every circumstance I have learned the secret [of facing

> *life], whether well-fed or going hungry, whether having an abundance or being in need. I can do all things [which He has called me to do] through Him who strengthens and empowers me [to fulfill His purpose—I am self-sufficient in Christ's sufficiency; I am ready for anything and equal to anything through Him who infuses me with inner strength and confident peace].*
>
> PHILIPPIANS 4:11–13 (AMP)

Have you ever been perfectly happy where you are while simultaneously dreaming of where you could go next? What happens when your natural gift for envisioning possibilities meets an invitation to simply . . . pause?

My parents arrived in the United States with just their suitcases, five children, and dreams bigger than our first cramped apartment. They chased the American dream with the kind of relentless hope that sees dignity in every honest job—and I mean *any.*

My father spent long stretches working the conveyor belts at the Coca-Cola® factory, eight hours of bottles rushing past in an endless parade. I'm pretty sure he could identify every Coke® bottle size in his sleep. Later, he did laundry for a hospital. You can imagine what that looked and smelled like, trying to cleanse the weight of other people's stories that clung to those sheets and scrubs.

My mother cleaned hotel rooms during one season, where guests left behind more than just unmade beds—sometimes tips, sometimes messes that tested her resolve. When the recession hit particularly hard, she became a waitress, serving tables with quiet grace—even when customers weren't kind to someone with an accent. Some asked her to repeat herself, again and again. Sometimes it was genuine confusion. Sometimes, it felt like a test of her patience. They rarely acknowledged the quiet miracle: she was speaking more languages than most of them had ever tried to learn.

Through it all, my parents never complained. Between them, across all these different seasons, they created a masterclass in resilience that no textbook could teach. Their sacrifices weren't abstract concepts—they were alarm clocks set for 4:00 a.m., uniforms that carried the scent of industrial soap and kitchen grease, and hands that bore the evidence of work that built our future one shift at a time. Every dollar represented a dream deferred for us.

I remember my first job as a waitress—coming home to count my tips at the kitchen table with my mother, then watching her tuck those crumpled bills away to help pay down the credit card debt that was quietly supporting us through the recession.

We learned early that love looks like sacrifice, and sacrifice demands a response. Whether your parents crossed oceans or crossed towns, worked factories or offices, most of us know that feeling—the weight of wanting to make someone's investment in us worthwhile.

Those humble beginnings made me a collector of achievements, always reaching for the next degree, the next opportunity, the next proof that all those early morning shifts and late-night worries had purpose. My pursuit of higher education stretched on like a marathon with no finish line in sight. There was always another goal, another mountain to climb, another way to say "thank you" through accomplishment.

From our earliest married days, I was the family dreamer-in-chief, always plotting our next educational conquest. "What about that master's program?" I'd ask my husband over morning coffee, my eyes already seeing possibilities stretching ahead of us. Coffee-stained textbooks competed for space with baby bottles on our kitchen counter.

Then came the season when our house transformed into what can only be described as a creative explosion. Cotton balls in every color imaginable were scattered across our living room table as I worked on design projects, filling in silhouettes with the precision of a surgeon and the mess of a toddler. Our vacuum cleaner probably thought it had entered some kind of crafting war zone.

My husband became my unexpected creative partner. He brainstormed advertisement slogans with me, debated font choices with the seriousness of a typography expert (he may have secretly wondered how he'd become a design consultant overnight), and somehow managed to hold steady while I wielded welding tools to create wire figures in our limited space.

Our kitchen table pulled double duty as a dining surface and art studio. Toddler gear shared counter space with design supplies that multiplied faster than we could contain them. Those early years were a beautiful tangle of dual late-night study sessions, church activities, and creative projects that refused to respect the boundaries of our living space.

As our family kept growing, so did our need for space. The house that had once felt spacious now seemed to shrink around us daily. Time for the next move.

We settled into our new home with that satisfying feeling of having made it to the next level. When we needed some construction work done, I called one of our pastors whose family ran a local company. It seemed like a perfect fit—someone we trusted, fair pricing, and supporting our church family.

The estimate went smoothly, and as our pastor reached for the door handle, he stopped. He just paused at the threshold, his hand resting on the door frame. I watched as his eyes swept across our foyer—taking in the gleaming floors, the fresh paint, the careful touches that made this house feel like home. And then I watched something shift in his expression. A thoughtfulness I hadn't expected.

When he turned back to me, his voice carried the weight of someone who'd learned a few things I hadn't.

"This is a really nice house," he said, his words coming slowly, deliberately. "Can you see yourself being here, watching your children grow, enjoying it—for a long time?"

The question hung in the air between us. My answer came quickly, almost defensively. "Definitely." But something about his question made me pause. Because the truth was, this concept felt completely foreign.

He didn't move from the doorway. That thoughtful look deepened as he continued. "You know, it's common to see others chase after bigger houses and nicer cars. It's so easy to get swept up in the desire for more. But finding rest, staying put for a while and being content in what God has given you—there's a peace that comes with that."

My father had been a dreamer, both my parents valued aspirations, but settling down? Resting in what I had without simultaneously planning the next move? It felt almost counterintuitive. Pausing between goals? I wasn't quite sure what to make of this idea.

I loved our home and was genuinely grateful. But I'd never considered that contentment might mean stopping the constant mental motion toward what came next.

Standing there in my foyer, something clicked. I grasped the importance of allowing myself to land in a blessing and stay put for a while before thinking about my next goal. But my pastor's insight went deeper than that. It grounded me in the necessity of balancing ambitions with rest, aspirations with satisfaction, reaching with contentment.

It was like someone had given me permission to exhale.

Over the years, this truth has anchored me when my goals have started running ahead of my actual capacity. That morning at my front door marked the beginning of a gentler way of living—learning to slow my pace just a bit, to strive a little less. When I started balancing my dreams with my real abilities and limitations, something beautiful happened. My life found its rhythm.

Instead of always leaning toward the next thing, I began to notice what was already here. Instead of measuring my worth by my next achievement, I started celebrating what I had already accomplished.

As our family has continued to grow, so has that familiar itch for more space. More bedrooms, more storage, more room to breathe. The old restlessness creeps back in. But instead of immediately house-hunting, I find myself doing something different—rearranging furniture with fresh eyes, tackling that long-overdue remodeling project, discovering space I didn't know we had by purging. Through these small transformations, I've been learning the surprising value of working with what's already here.

So instead of scrolling through real estate listings, I close the laptop. I walk through our home differently. I see it not as a stepping stone, but as a beautiful space where my children and grandchildren's laughter echoes off these very walls.

Contentment, I'm learning, isn't a destination. It's a daily choice to see abundance in what's already here. Ultimately, it's about living joyfully, choosing satisfaction in any situation, without giving up on our dreams. I'm learning to wait for the Lord's perfect timing before chasing new visions.

For any of us caught between gratitude and ambition, it starts with a simple shift—changing how we see our circumstances when our hearts need grounding. Because sometimes the most profound growth happens not when we're reaching for more, but when we're learning to be fully present with enough.

Father,

Thank You for the gentle wisdom that comes through unexpected conversations and ordinary moments.

Thank You for being the God of both dreams and rest, ambition and peace.

Teach my heart the difference between godly ambition and endless striving. When my dreams start to outrun my peace, slow me down. When restlessness whispers that I need more, anchor me in Your perfect provision.

Help me learn the sacred art of pausing—of resting in Your blessings long enough to savor and be content there. Remind me that contentment isn't giving up—it's trusting Your timing completely.

Give me eyes to see my current circumstances through Your perspective, finding joy in what is—while believing for what is to come.

Grant me the wisdom to know when to reach and when to rest, when to strive and when to simply breathe.

In Jesus' name, Amen.

> Sometimes the most profound growth happens not when we're reaching for more, but when we're learning to be fully present with enough.

A Moment of Reflection

1. When you look around your current circumstances—your home, relationships, or season of life—what blessings do you tend to overlook?

2. What would it look like to "land in a blessing and stay put for a while" in your current situation?

3. How might your present circumstances be preparing you for what God has ahead, even if you can't see the full picture yet?

4. *What dreams or goals are you chasing that might be keeping you from fully experiencing the goodness of where you are right now?*

____

____

____

____

5. *What drives your need to reach for the next goal before fully enjoying what you've already accomplished?*

____

____

____

____

6. *What would you need to release or surrender to find peace in the space between your dreams and your current reality?*

____

____

____

____

SECTION V

TRUSTING GOD'S PLAN means letting go of your tight grip on how things should unfold and embracing the sovereignty of His timing. It's realizing closed doors are not always losses, detours may not be setbacks, and learning that even when things don't unfold as you planned, He's always got your back.

27

His Hand in Mine

Life's journey rarely unfolds the way we expect—the road twists and turns, sometimes smooth, sometimes rough with potholes that jolt us into uncertainty. We've all felt that ache of loneliness, heard the whisper that maybe we've been left behind, listened to old lies echo louder than they should. But here's what remains true even when everything else feels unstable: God's promises don't waver. He will never leave us or forsake us.

> *"But I'll take the hand of those who don't know the way, who can't see where they're going . . . I'll be right there to show them what roads to take, make sure they don't fall into the ditch . . . sticking with them, not leaving them for a minute."*
>
> ISAIAH 42:16 (MSG)

Living just under thirty minutes from the vibrant heart of New York City made each visit an exhilarating adventure. The city's bustling streets were full of honking taxis, towering skyscrapers, and bustling sidewalks. On this particular weekend, the city air buzzed with urgency and anticipation.

It was Election Day for the upcoming president of our native country, Colombia. Campaign posters adorned buildings, and the yellow, blue, and red colored flags waved confidently on the city streets. The aroma of native street food mingled with the sounds of passionate, patriotic pedestrians, their voices rising above the city clamor. Their patriotism evident in their flag-colored attire.

At that time, my parents were recent immigrants to the United States, still toying with the idea of returning to their country of origin. They were proud Colombians who were concerned for the future of their country due to the civil war that was brewing there between the government and the far-left guerrilla groups. To my family, it was an important day to vote. As we neared the voting center the crowd waved banners, animated voices filled the air in lively debates, echoing their intense passion for politics.

The sea of people, ranging from the affluent to the homeless, stretched as far as the eye could see—each individual moving swiftly and purposefully in countless directions. As a little girl, my near to the ground view was limited to a vast vista of pant legs. Tugged along by my parents, I had no idea where I was going, why we needed to walk so fast, or who we were going to meet. It seemed like for every step my father took, I took four, my little steps striving to move in sync with his confident strides. In those days, at least where I grew up, children simply followed where they were led, asking no questions, just moving as quickly as their little legs could carry them.

I remember well, my small hand nestled within my father's strong, comforting grip, his veins prominently visible, anchoring me in the midst of all the chaos. It was my lifeline. That was where my focus rested. Somehow, it felt as if nothing else mattered.

I didn't need to know where I was going or what time we would arrive there. My father threaded me safely through the crowd of unfamiliar faces and curious situations, carefully guarding me every step of the way. He could be both fierce and gentle, demanding and protective. But in this moment, I only felt his strength. I felt safe. I glanced upwards, catching glimpses of his calm demeanor, feeling a sense of security. With his hand in mine, fear had no voice. Oh, what a trusting child I was.

> With his hand in mine, fear had no voice.

Walking hectic city streets, amidst clamor and chaos, while uncertain of my ultimate destination, mirrors my own life's journey. As much as I want to believe I'm in control, I realize none of us truly are. We never know what awaits us around the corner. Yet, holding onto God's hand reassures us we are never alone, never abandoned. No matter how overwhelming life becomes, He walks beside us through every unexpected twist and turn, offering us His steadfast presence and offering safety, protection, and security we can find nowhere else.

Father,

When I stand amidst life's crowded streets, overwhelmed by its noise, confused by its pace, and uncertain of where my path leads, I thank You for sending Your Holy Spirit as my companion and comforter. Like a child's hand in the protective grasp of a loved one, let me feel the security of Your presence guiding me through the chaos.

In moments when anxiety whispers its lies and abandonment casts its shadow, help me focus not on the sea of uncertainty that surrounds me, but on the unwavering truth that You hold me. Make Your presence as real to me as a loving hand that anchors a child through unfamiliar crowds.

When I cannot see what's ahead of me, and fear tries to overcome me, remind me that You see the entire journey. May I learn to trust You in uncertainty and find rest in knowing that You are leading me.

Amen.

A Moment of Reflection

1. *What moments remind you that God stays close, even when answers come slowly?*

____

____

____

____

2. *Is there an area of your life where you're struggling to believe God will protect you or show up in time?*

____

____

____

____

3. *"With his hand in mine, fear had no voice." Is there an area in your life where fear is speaking loudly right now?*

____

____

____

____

4. *In what area of your life do you need to shift your focus from the situation to the hand that's holding yours?*

5. *What fears or beliefs make it hard for you to pause and enjoy the present moment without planning what comes next?*

6. *What lies have taken root in your heart that convince you you're walking alone? How have these falsehoods affected your ability to trust God's presence in uncertain times?*

28

When Closed Doors Open Oceans

Difficult situations can blind us with hopelessness, appearing as dead ends. Yet, God uses these trials to redirect us, unveiling new, unexpected opportunities.

> *And we know that God causes all things to work together for good to those who love God, to those who are called according to His purpose.*
>
> ROMANS 8:28 (NASB)

It's fascinating how certain events align to bring your dreams to life. Becoming a travel agent had captured my imagination since my teenage years. In the early days of marriage, my husband and I entertained the possibility of launching our own travel agency, but with three children filling our home with laughter and responsibilities, our focus naturally shifted elsewhere. However, life took an unexpected turn when my husband's career screeched to a halt. Multiple injuries from years of hard, physical labor had taken their toll.

As a homeschooling mom, my problem-solving instincts immediately kicked into high gear. My mind raced, unraveling solutions and clearing mental hurdles one by one. My parents lived with us then, a blessing that allowed them to help with our children, while I focused on generating much-needed income.

As I contemplated working options, I reached for the newspaper, scanning ads, and stumbled upon one that caught my eye. The words seemed to glow from the page *Travel Agents Needed for Cruise Line. Will Train. Being bilingual is a plus.* Excitement bubbled up inside me as I rushed to my husband, newspaper clutched in my hand. "Look! I could do this to support us financially while we navigate your job transition."

Deep down, I harbored a secret hope—perhaps employee benefits would include cruise discounts for my family. We had already experienced the joy of cruising several times, each offering amazing adventures and creating treasured memories. My husband had earned a cruise through his exceptional work performance, and my father-in-law had generously treated us to a few voyages as a couple. The sparkle in my husband's eyes during those brief escapes from routine had been magical. Together, we often dreamed of someday sailing as a family, sharing these wonderful experiences with our children.

After reviewing the ad again, my fingers trembled slightly as I completed the application. To my astonishment and delight, I was hired for a sales position and stepped into an adventure I hadn't expected but somehow felt destined for. The benefits at the cruise line exceeded my wildest expectations. As a travel agent, I could contribute financially to my family, book dream vacations for others, leverage my bilingual abilities, and most importantly, turn our cruising dreams into reality. It was an enticing blend of professional fulfillment and family adventure—a real win-win situation.

Joining Premier Cruise Lines came with more enticing perks. My training culminated in an employee weekend cruise—a nice bonus, but not what I really desired. My true longing was for a cruise with my family. However, after three months of service, I could take my family on a weekend cruise to the Bahamas, with half-priced excursions. In addition, after nine months with Premier, an even greater treasure was unlocked, a week-long cruise for my family at no cost, offering us the chance to create lasting memories together.

Working at Premier became my all-time favorite job. Arranging trips for others connected people to happy vacations. Reaching sales goals built my confidence one call at a time. Selling wasn't about numbers on a page. It was discovering strengths I never knew I possessed, stretching beyond self-imposed limitations into new territories of ability.

Ultimately, my hard work paid off spectacularly, allowing us to embark on two unforgettable family cruises. These trips turned into the best vacations we could have imagined gifting our children.

The turquoise waters of the Caribbean stretched endlessly around us as we sailed. Watching my children's faces light up as they swam with dolphins was priceless. I will never forget hearing my daughter's muffled squeals of delight resonating through the water, as she discovered neon fish and underwater wonders through her snorkel mask.

Ancient Mayan ruins in Mexico transported us through time, stone pathways whispered stories from centuries past. These journeys marked our children's first steps beyond U.S. borders. Our shared adventures didn't merely broaden horizons; they wove our family closer together, creating a tapestry of memories we still unfold and admire years later.

It's interesting how we often fixate on closed doors, paralyzed by fear and uncertainty. We forget that God uses these precise circumstances to reveal new opportunities we would never have considered otherwise.

And we know that God causes all things to work together for good to those who love God, to those who are called according to His purpose.

ROMANS 8:28 (NASB)

Praying for our desires forms the first bridge between dreams and reality. God invites us to share our deepest wishes with Him—not because He needs information, but because He treasures connection. He hears heart-whispers even before we speak them aloud. Although I don't remember specifically praying about taking our family cruising, He knew I carried this desire within me.

It's also true that many times bringing dreams to life requires action alongside prayer. By establishing goals and pursuing them with determination, we activate faith and unlock doors to divine possibilities. Webster defines a "pipe dream" as an illusory or fantastic hope. The transformation from wishful thinking to realized dreams happens through creating solid plans, taking purposeful steps, and maintaining discipline even when motivation wanes. This practice turns vague hopes into clear destinations, with

> It's interesting how we often fixate on closed doors, paralyzed by fear and uncertainty. We forget that God uses these precise circumstances to reveal new opportunities we would never have considered otherwise.

faith illuminating each step forward—creating a beautiful partnership between our human effort and God's divine provision.

When my husband lost his job, it unexpectedly opened the door for me to turn an improbable dream into reality. As I built my confidence and excelled in sales, I discovered that our visions often materialize when we partner with God to bring them to life.

Human nature often waits passively, forgetting even to pray. But when we trust God to guide our paths and fulfill our desires, He often shows up with gifts surpassing our imagination. What began as a painful job loss blossomed into adventures that continue enriching our family story—proof that God specializes in redirecting dead ends into detours of unexpected blessing.

> God specializes in redirecting dead ends into detours of unexpected blessing.

Father,

My heart overflows with gratitude knowing You cherish even my unspoken wishes. I bring before You the dreams I carry—some merely whispers in my quiet moments, others burning brightly within me. Nothing is too small to bring before You, and no dream is insignificant to You.

I place each hope in Your loving hands, these treasures of my heart that sometimes feel too fragile to share elsewhere. How precious is Your attention, Lord—the way You listen when others might drift away, the way You find meaning in what the world might dismiss.

How mind-blowing it is to think that You—who set stars in motion—delights in my voice, that you lean in close when I speak, finding joy in our intimate conversations. Thank You for treasuring our time together.

Amen.

A Moment of Reflection

1. *Think of a time God gave you something you never even prayed for. What did that teach you about how well He knows you?*

____

____

____

____

2. *How has God previously worked circumstances together for your good, even when the situation initially appeared devastating? What did this teach you about His character?*

____

____

____

____

3. *In what area of your life are you currently "staring at a closed door" instead of looking for the new opportunity God might be revealing?*

____

____

____

4. *What new abilities or gifts might God be developing in you through your current challenges?*

____

____

____

____

5. *Has God been nudging your heart toward a dream that requires you to create plans, take steps, and partner with Him intentionally?*

____

____

____

____

6. *Is there a desire you've been afraid to voice to God because it feels too big or too selfish?*

____

____

____

____

29

Rocks In My Backpack

What if the very tasks we resist are the ones quietly shaping us, chiseling character in silence, carving strength through repetition? What if the mundane moments we try to avoid are sacred invitations? Each act of faithful stewardship becomes a stone in the backpack, not to weigh us down, but to build the muscle we'll need for the climb ahead.

> *"The one who faithfully manages the little he has been given will be promoted and trusted with greater responsibilities. But those who cheat with the little they have been given will not be considered trustworthy to receive more."*
>
> LUKE 16:10 (TPT)

"Don't think about it. It just needs to be done. Just do it." No softness, no preamble. Just truth that went straight in.

My mother's simple words dissolved years of inner conflict about mopping floors. No profound wisdom, no lengthy lecture—just

> What if the very tasks we resist are the ones quietly shaping us, chiseling character in silence, carving strength through repetition?

straightforward advice that changed my perspective on how to do menial tasks I did not enjoy.

There I was, rattling off my household duties to my mother like any young wife might—this needs cleaning, that needs organizing. I never intended to dissect why I hated mopping so much. But mothers have a way of hearing what we don't say out loud. Her straightforward response to my grumbling surprised me. I opened my mouth, then closed it again, then fumbled for words. Truthfully, I had no valid excuse other than it seemed more boring than any other chore. It wasn't even that the area I needed to mop was large. I just didn't like it—no rhyme or reason.

That brief exchange with my mother shifted something in me—suddenly I was examining my feelings about housework in ways I never had before. Did I not enjoy housework? No, it wasn't that. From a young age, I took on the daily household chores to lighten my mother's burden. Although my mother never complained, I could see the toll years of hard labor had taken on her. I noticed how she moved a little slower in the evenings after hours hunched over her workbench. Most of all, I saw the weariness in her eyes after a day spent focusing on tiny circuits to solder.

Keeping the house tidy became my quiet way of easing her load—a small gift I could offer without saying a word. I loved seeing her eyes light up when she noticed the freshly vacuumed carpets and neatly folded laundry. It felt like the least I could do, knowing the weight she carried. Her expression reminded me that love often speaks loudest through service.

As soon as she arrived home, my mother would dive into the kitchen, crafting elaborate dinners from scratch. The scent of freshly chopped vegetables, finely minced garlic, and onions softly sizzling on the stove filled the air with a comforting aroma. It was the fragrance of love. Her commitment to preparing nutritious meals was unwavering, a reflection of her nurturing nature.

> "Don't think about it. It just needs to be done. Just do it."

Thinking back to those days, I realized housework wasn't something I typically dreaded. Organizing and dusting were soothing routines and the rhythmic back-and-forth of the vacuum created a meditative state where my thoughts could wander. However, mopping was a different story. For some reason, mopping was something I did not enjoy at all. But with my mother's simple advice, I never procrastinated or dreaded mopping the floor again.

Later that day, my mother's words stuck with me. I thought about all the tasks she'd done over the years without complaint. Whether waking before dawn to work, sewing, welding, housekeeping in hotels, or waiting tables, she did it all. She even sold various items like gold jewelry, clothes, and custom jewelry, besides her full-time job to bring in extra income. Though I could see the weariness on her face, she never procrastinated or complained about the tedious tasks she had to do to keep our household going.

Before we can reframe drudgery, we need to name it. Drudgery is the kind of work that feels dull, repetitive, and draining. It's the stuff we often avoid—chores that don't spark joy or creativity, but still need to be done.

The fact is, we all have a little drudgery to tackle. What tasks come to mind for you that are boring, dull, and unpleasant? For me, it's cleaning the toilets, washing a sink full of dirty dishes while everyone else is visiting during a family gathering, or going through and organizing a desk covered in paperwork. These tasks do nothing to boost my ego and have no great everlasting tangible reward. If you think about it, drudgery involves tasks we are required to perform repeatedly.

In a world filled with distractions and endless entertainment, it's easy to find reasons to put off doing the mundane tasks. So, why is it important to incorporate drudgery into our everyday lives? Does engaging in menial work hold any value? How can we overcome the dread of these seemingly meaningless activities?

The first step is recognizing the value of drudgery. Like so many things in life, it comes down to how we choose to see what's in front of us. I've learned that the mundane holds more power than I gave it credit for. These daily tasks I once saw as drudgery? They're quietly building character, teaching patience, creating rhythm in ways I'm only beginning to understand.

Doing the menial is actually a stepping stone towards maturity. Achieving goals often requires going through drudgery. It acts as a doorway to bigger and better opportunities. In fact, confronting drudgery leads to a clear mind—a blank canvas for creative flow.

My mother's insight that day echoed something deeper. Suddenly I could see what had been right in front of me all along. It's our faithfulness in the everyday that prepares us for something bigger and better. It's doing the mundane with a good attitude that builds character.

Our ability to steward well is tested in the responsibilities we are given every day. Before we are trusted with what we are called to do, we must first learn to do what calls us. Often, what we need is an attitude adjustment. Drudgery and dread must be replaced in our lives by an attitude of love and service.

Colossians 3:23 (NASB1995) says:

Whatever you do, do your work heartily, as for the Lord rather than for men.

Our ability to steward well is tested in the responsibilities we are given every day.

When we see our tasks as drudgery, as boring and meaningless work, it drains our energy and blocks our progress. It acts as a barrier, stalling the momentum we need to advance. Shifting our attitude from dread to joy can be empowering.

Drudgery weighs us down before we even begin, like rocks filling an invisible backpack we carry. Each negative thought adds another stone, becoming so heavy we can barely move. It traps us in a pit of hopelessness, robbing us of motivation and keeping us stuck. We stop growing. We forget we have a choice.

But what if we could learn to see our backpack differently? What if, instead of dreading the mundane work, I could let those repetitive chores build something in me? Every time I wash one more dish, mop one more corner, fold one more load of clothes, maybe my invisible backpack is actually making me stronger for the greater heights I'm meant to climb.

Jesus sets the example.

Therefore, since we have so great a cloud of witnesses surrounding us, let us also lay aside every encumbrance and the sin which so easily entangles us, and let us run with endurance the race that is set before us, fixing our eyes on Jesus, the author and perfecter of faith, who for the joy set

before Him endured the cross, despising the shame, and has sat down at the right hand of the throne of God."

HEBREWS 12:1–2 (NASB1995)

I'm starting to see that in my daily choice to embrace these necessary tasks, no matter how mundane, there's something deeper happening. Jesus modeled this when he washed feet and fed the hungry, showing how humble service paves the way to divine purpose. When I empty my backpack of procrastination and simply do what needs to be done, I'm not just completing chores. I'm participating in something meaningful. These faithful moments are changing something within me, clearing a path I couldn't see before. The tasks I once dreaded are no longer obstacles. They're invitations. And each one is shaping me for the climb ahead.

Heavenly Father,

How grateful I am that You strengthen my hands for the work before me today. When tasks feel mundane and insignificant, help me remember they're not just chores to check off—they're shaping my character and building discipline for what You have ahead.

Holy Spirit, when my soul grows weary under the weight of daily responsibilities, whisper reminders of Your grace. Build my endurance. Replace my reluctance with joy, my procrastination with purpose.

Father, I praise You for the wisdom hidden in discipline. Thank You that as I steward these seemingly insignificant tasks with excellence, You're crafting a foundation for greater Kingdom work. Not for my glory, but for Yours alone.

May each mundane moment today become an offering of worship, a testimony to Your transforming presence in the ordinary corners of my life. In Jesus' name, Amen.

A Moment of Reflection

1. **What simple truth has God been trying to speak into your life that you might be overcomplicating?**

2. **What specific task could become a prayer offering to God today?**

3. **In what areas of your life have you been viewing necessary tasks as drudgery rather than service?**

4. *How might your view of "menial" tasks shift if you saw them as spiritual weight training—building character and blessing others?*

____

____

____

____

5. *Do you see mundane tasks as burdens holding you back or as weights building your spiritual muscles?*

____

____

____

____

6. *What calling have you been minimizing, and how might that be blocking the creative flow God wants to release in your life?*

____

____

____

____

30

Papi, Please Let's Take the Long Way!

The timeless struggle—our hearts long for shortcuts when God asks us to walk the longer path. We all face seasons when following God's timeline feels painfully slow, unnecessarily winding. The craving for immediate results, instant wisdom, and effortless success runs deep in our human nature. But what if those frustrating detours, the ones that make us grip the steering wheel tighter, actually contain the lessons we need most?

> *And not only* **this,** *but [with joy] let us exult in our sufferings and rejoice in our hardships, knowing that hardship (distress, pressure, trouble) produces patient endurance; and endurance, proven character (spiritual maturity); and proven character, hope* **and** *confident assurance [of eternal salvation].*
>
> ROMANS 5:3–4 (AMP)

267

The old aqua station wagon slowed at yet another unfamiliar intersection—the result of my father's latest "shortcut." A familiar knot tightened in my stomach as tension hung thick in our family car, like summer humidity before a storm. My father's eyes darted across the street signs, worry and stubborn pride written across his face.

"I don't understand what happened," he exclaimed, his voice rising with exasperation. He refused to acknowledge that his shortcut had left us hopelessly disoriented once again. "That gas station attendant gave me completely wrong directions!"

My mother's quiet sigh spoke volumes. These deflections—his inability to admit we were lost—had become our family's unintentional prayer for patience. It was a recurring ritual that always preceded tears, arguments, and arriving late, if we made it to our destination at all.

Oh, what we would have given for a GPS back then. In those days, going anywhere became an unplanned adventure the moment my father decided to try a quicker way. I can still hear the rustling of rarely-unfolded maps, see my mother's tense shoulders as she suggested alternate routes only to be met with my father's frustrated "I know where I'm going!" The weight of inevitable disappointment settled over us all as every time, our simple trip morphed into an epic journey to nowhere.

Trip after trip, my siblings and I grew more bored in the backseat, our destination seeming to drift farther away with each wrong turn. Questions bubbled inside me. *Why do we always have to be late? Why can't we take the long way like everyone else? Why does every trip have to get so complicated?*

No matter how often we got lost, my father's confidence that a shortcut would be best never seemed to waiver. His well-intended alternatives inevitably led to unnecessary stress. Regardless of how hard he tried to get us there earlier by utilizing short-cuts, it just did not happen. At just six years old, I already understood a truth many adults struggle to grasp—shortcuts rarely deliver what they promise. What looks like a faster route often becomes a frustrating detour, consuming more time than the reliable path would have taken.

One afternoon, when the car slowed near an unfamiliar turn, I found courage I didn't know I had. "Papi, please don't take a shortcut," I said with surprising boldness. "I would really rather go the long way."

The shocked silence that followed taught me something profound about speaking truth, even when you're small. However, seeing the fallacy of my father's shortcuts still didn't teach me to completely avoid taking them as an adult. Some lessons are only learned the hard way.

The reality is that most of us naturally lean toward shortcuts. Waiting tests our patience, and this impatience has been part of human nature since the very beginning. Yet there is something about "the process" or "the wait" that God values far more than we do. There are treasures discovered on the long journey that shortcuts simply cannot teach.

> Yet there is something about "the process" or "the wait" that God values far more than we do. There are treasures discovered on the long journey that shortcuts simply cannot teach.

Scripture shows us this pattern repeatedly. In Genesis, Satan tempts Eve with a shortcut—instant wisdom through the forbidden fruit. But the consequences were devastating.

Jesus also faced the "shortcut temptation" in the wilderness, when the enemy tempted Him three times at His weakest point. Matthew 4:1–10 (NIV) says:

Then Jesus was led by the Spirit into the wilderness to be tempted by the devil. After fasting forty days and forty nights, he was hungry. The tempter came to him and said, "If you are the Son of God, tell these stones to become bread."

Jesus answered, "It is written: 'Man shall not live on bread alone, but on every word that comes from the mouth of God.'"

Then the devil took him to the holy city and had him stand on the highest point of the temple. "If you are the Son of God," he said, "throw yourself down. For it is written:

"'He will command his angels concerning you, and they will lift you up in their hands, so that you will not strike your foot against a stone.'"

Jesus answered him, "It is also written: 'Do not put the Lord your God to the test.'"

Again, the devil took him to a very high mountain and showed him all the kingdoms of the world and their splendor. "All this I will give you," he said, "if you will bow down and worship me."

Jesus said to him, "Away from me, Satan! For it is written: 'Worship the Lord your God, and serve him only.'"

You know what strikes me about Jesus's temptation in the wilderness? Satan dangled the ultimate shortcut—all the kingdoms without the cross. But Jesus chose the harder road—the road of love, that led to our salvation.

It's easy to say we value something, but our choices under pressure? That's where we discover what we actually treasure.

The truth is, all those frustrating delays and detours are actually doing something in us. When I'm forced to slow down, that's when I start asking the hard questions about my motivations and reactions. It's funny how waiting can reveal things about ourselves we'd rather not see.

But what do we do with the in-between times—those seasons when we're forced to wait for God's timing? I've discovered there's a difference between just enduring a delay and actually paying attention during it. Active waiting isn't standing still in a period of delay, drumming our fingers impatiently until time passes. It's like mining for gold—carefully sifting through our circumstances to discover what God is revealing in the midst of the wait.

Whether we've stumbled into a difficult season or God has purposefully led us there, these circumstances carry divine purpose. Sometimes the soil of our hearts needs time to be properly prepared. There are always seeds of wisdom woven into our waiting that we might otherwise miss in our rushing.

In the end, embracing the journey rather than grasping for shortcuts isn't merely about arriving somewhere—it's about who you become through it. Every challenge that stretches our faith, every season of waiting that feels endless—these are the very places where God shapes our character with the gentle patience of a master craftsman.

> Active waiting isn't standing still in a period of delay, drumming our fingers impatiently until time passes. It's like mining for gold—carefully sifting through our circumstances to discover what God is revealing in the midst of the wait.

The six-year-old me who pleaded, "Papi, please let's go the long way," had stumbled upon something I'm still learning. The shortcuts we crave often bypass the very experiences designed to transform us. When we surrender to God's timing and trust His navigation, the path may wind longer than we'd choose, but the views along the way—and the person we become in the traveling—make every extra mile worthwhile.

The greatest destination isn't a place at all, but the person God is shaping you to become through the beautiful, frustrating, necessary process of the longer road.

Loving Father,

In my hurry and haste, when my heart grows impatient with Your timeline—slow me. Help me see with different eyes what You're doing in my waiting.

I recognize my tendency to seek shortcuts. My restless reaching for what seems faster and easier. Forgive me for the times I've tried to bypass Your process, rushing past the very transformation You intended to happen.

You know how I struggle when the path winds longer than I'd choose. How the questions rise within me. How fear whispers that I'll never arrive.

Plant my feet firmly in Your timing—not mine. When I'm tempted to force doors open, remind me that Your delays are not denials but invitations to deeper trust.

In the stretching seasons, in the holy delays, may I discover You there. May I recognize the treasures hidden in the longer road.

Give me courage, like a child's simple wisdom, to say, "Father, let's take the long way."

Help me realize that the journey itself is shaping me—and the destination is becoming more like You.

In Jesus' name, Amen.

A Moment of Reflection

1. *How do you typically respond when God's timeline feels painfully slow? Do you find yourself growing frustrated, or can you trust the process?*

2. *What "shortcut temptations" do you face most often in your spiritual journey? How might these shortcuts bypass important growth?*

3. *Consider your current season of waiting. What might God be preparing in the soil of your heart during this time?*

4. *Instead of just enduring this delay, what if you started looking for what God is revealing in the midst of it? What are you noticing?*

____

____

____

____

5. *What specific wisdom or growth is available to you right now on this "long way" that taking a shortcut would cause you to miss?*

____

____

____

____

6. *What are you most afraid of missing out on by staying on God's timeline? What does that fear tell you?*

____

____

____

____

31

His Wedding Gift

In those moments when anxiety grips our hearts and prayers seem to go unanswered, God invites us to shift our focus from what we lack to what we can trust. When life's uncertainties threaten to overwhelm us, Scripture offers an anchor for our anxious thoughts. Our greatest challenges may actually be the perfect canvas for experiencing God's intervention in ways we never imagined possible.

> *Finally, brothers and sisters, whatever is true, whatever is honorable, whatever is right, whatever is pure, whatever is lovely, whatever is commendable, if there is any excellence and if anything worthy of praise, think about these things.*
>
> PHILIPPIANS 4:8 (NASB)

"We're getting married in four weeks. Where are we going to live?"

Everything was falling into place—the dress, the flowers, the rings. Four years of waiting, dreaming, planning, but despite our best efforts, we still didn't have a home. I stared at our dwindling housing options. We'd already lost one down payment. My parents' warning about that money pit had saved us from one disaster, but left us facing another—where would we live?

> Our greatest challenges may actually be the perfect canvas for experiencing God's intervention in ways we never imagined possible.

As college students juggling textbooks and timecards, we approached our finances with careful intention. My fiancé worked full-time while I balanced part-time hours with classes. We'd saved a respectable down payment, but we were determined to be wise with our future.

"You could qualify for more," the mortgage broker told us, sliding a paper with a much higher number than we applied for across his desk. We exchanged glances and shook our heads—we wanted a home we could afford comfortably, not one that would keep us awake at night.

Still, our prudence narrowed our options considerably in a seller's market. Each night, I prayed, wondering if my words were reaching beyond the ceiling. Would our first home together be my old bedroom in my parents' house? How do you trust God's timing when your own deadline refuses to budge? The clock ticked louder each day—was God hearing it too?

With every house we toured, hope rose and fell like a roller coaster. The calendar pages flipped mercilessly toward our wedding date.

Back then, closing on a house required at least a month of paperwork shuffling—no convenient computer clicks to speed things along. We were precisely one month away from saying "I do," with nowhere to go after saying it.

My stomach knotted at the thought of having no home to begin our life together in. My parents had generously offered their spare room, but the image of starting our marriage under their roof made my heart sink. Their small house, already crowded with life and love, wasn't where we wanted to hang our first picture frame together.

My mother noticed the worry etched across my forehead. Having embraced faith only a few years earlier, we were spiritual toddlers learning to walk with Scripture as our guide. The idea was still revolutionary to us that God's promises weren't just beautiful words on ancient pages but living truths we could speak over our circumstances. Learning to take verses and make them personal, to confess them over our fears and dreams, felt like discovering a secret language between heaven and earth.

One afternoon, my mother found me staring blankly at rental listings. "I have to share something with you." Mami's voice held that unmistakable tone that meant she'd been praying about my situation. She sat beside me, Bible in hand, her voice soft but steady as she read Philippians 4:6–8 from the Amplified Version.

> *Do not be anxious or worried about anything, but in everything [every circumstance and situation] by prayer and petition with thanksgiving, continue to make your [specific] requests known to God. And the peace of God [that peace which reassures the heart, that peace] which transcends all*

understanding, [that peace which] stands guard over your hearts and your minds in Christ Jesus [is yours].

Finally, believers, whatever is true, whatever is honorable and worthy of respect, whatever is right and confirmed by God's word, whatever is pure and wholesome, whatever is lovely and brings peace, whatever is admirable and of good repute; if there is any excellence, if there is anything worthy of praise, think continually on these things [center your mind on them, and implant them in your heart].

When I reminded her we were down to three weeks—an impossible timeline—she didn't back down. "That's exactly when God likes to show up," my mother said firmly. "It's time to let the worry go."

Her conviction was contagious.

I read the verse again. Then again. Something inside me exhaled as I read those words. With each repetition, worry lost ground, replaced by peace. I went back to the beginning, this time letting each phrase settle into the anxious spaces of my heart.

Then I dared to believe.

From that moment on, when worry approached like an unwelcome visitor, I'd close my eyes and recite those verses, building a fortress around my thoughts. Instead of mentally decorating a home we didn't have, I began thanking God for our new home—wherever and whatever it might be. The impossible timeline still stared at me, but something inside me had shifted from panic to promise.

Then it happened.

Not far from our parents' homes stood a cluster of apartments, barely three years old, now being converted into condominiums. Each had two bedrooms, access to a community swimming pool, and a price tag that didn't make our bank account weep. Until that moment, "condominium" hadn't appeared on our radar. We had envisioned a traditional house with a yard and a picket fence.

But as we stepped inside, something shifted. The newness of the condos meant freedom from the repair costs that older homes demanded. As we walked through, I could already see our furniture placed just so, picture frames finding their perfect spots on freshly painted walls. It fit—not just our budget, but us.

The paperwork that had crawled at a snail's pace suddenly shifted into high gear when we chose the condo route. Miraculously, three weeks later—just days before our wedding—we slid the key into our very first lock.

Freshly painted and beautifully renovated, it felt like stepping into a dream we hadn't dared to imagine. Beyond our wildest expectations, we had amenities we could never have afforded in a traditional home—a sparkling pool, a clubhouse that would become the backdrop for precious memories, including my first baby shower a year later.

Through that experience, I came to see that God's provision rarely stops at *just enough*—He finds joy in being extravagant. When we place our trust in God's hands, He doesn't just meet our needs—He exceeds our dreams.

Years ago, a pastor shared something that forever changed how I understand both faith and fear. He said they're both filmmakers in the theater of our minds. Fear directs horror films—vivid scenes of everything that could go wrong. Faith produces hope-filled documentaries—stories of God's goodness unfolding, frame by frame.

Both demand our attention. Both feel real. The question is, *which movie are you going to watch?*

The differences lie in how each movie engages our senses. Fear magnifies disaster until it's all you can see—pushing to the front of the line, screaming for immediate attention. Faith, however, sits quietly in the waiting room of your heart, patient until you're ready to rest and listen. She doesn't force you to see her vision. Instead, she offers you a choice, extending to you the opportunity to create dreams God can transform into realities.

When God promised Abraham descendants like stars and sand, He did something brilliant—He gave Abraham visual anchors he could touch and see every single day. Sand slipping through his fingers at the shoreline. Stars scattered across the night sky like diamonds on black velvet. Twenty-four hours of visible reminders kept God's promise before Abraham's eyes. God built His promise into Abraham's daily routine, making faith as tangible as the ground beneath his feet.

Sometimes multiple enemies line up to sabotage our faith. First comes fear—raw and primal. The Israelites feared the giants in the Promised Land, convinced they'd be crushed like grasshoppers (Numbers 13:32–33). David's brothers feared he'd be slaughtered by Goliath (1 Samuel 17). The disciples feared the storm would sink their boat while Jesus slept peacefully (Mark 4:35–41).

Then doubt slips in with its whispered questions. "Did God really say?" just as the serpent hissed to Eve in the garden (Genesis 3:1).

But when fear and doubt need backup, big brother Logic steps in, casting shadows on God's promises with charts and calculations. Sarah's logic said ninety-year-old wombs don't conceive (Genesis 18:11). Moses' logic argued that stutterers can't lead nations (Exodus 4:10–12). The disciples' logic calculated that five loaves couldn't possibly feed five thousand hungry people (Matthew 14:13–21). Each time, human reasoning tried to edit God's promises with a red pen. But God's math has never followed earthly equations. What God speaks, He fulfills. What He promises, He delivers—often in packages we never thought to look for.

Sometimes the home you need isn't the one you've been searching for. And sometimes, the impossible deadline is precisely when God does His most beautiful work.

Lord,

When anxiety tries to hold me captive—whispering doubts, clouding my vision, convincing me that You are not listening when I speak, that You don't hear what I need—I choose to look away.

Teach me to exchange my fears for Your promises. I choose to trust Your perfect timing over my own calculations.

What God speaks, He fulfills. What He promises, He delivers—often in packages we never thought to look for.

Help me see the upcoming miracle, not the logic that tries to convince me that my faith is a failure. I surrender my grip on how I think things should unfold. Replace my worry with gratitude for what You're already preparing in the unseen places.

Give me daily anchors for my faith, like You gave Abraham the sand and stars.

Thank You for being the God who doesn't just give us enough but delights in exceeding our dreams in ways we never imagined.

Help me shift my gaze from what I lack to the One I can trust.
In Jesus' name, Amen.

A Moment of Reflection

1. *Think about a time when God's provision exceeded your expectations. Did His gift come in packaging you never thought to look for?*

____

____

____

____

2. *What Scripture or promise from God serves as your anchor when your faith is being challenged?*

____

____

____

____

3. *What specific situation in your life right now has an "impossible timeline" that's making you anxious? What story is your fear telling you about how it will end?*

____

____

____

4. *When you face that impossible circumstance, are you trying to edit God's promises with human logic? What would it look like to let go of that logic?*

____

____

____

____

5. *Which movie are you currently watching more often—fear's horror film of everything that could go wrong, or faith's documentary of God's goodness? What does that reveal about where your trust really lies?*

____

____

____

____

6. *When anxiety whispers that God isn't listening, what specific truths about His character can you choose to look towards?*

____

____

____

____

ABOUT THE AUTHOR

ARLENE MANCILLA COOK spent years searching for the secret—how to live well, love deeply, and navigate life's challenges with grace. She discovered God had been speaking all along through everyday moments, offering not formulas but friendship, not religion but relationship. A Colombian American storyteller with a Doctorate of Ministry Leadership and master's degrees in Ministry and Clinical Mental Health Counseling, she invites others to find the sacred thread of God's love running through the fabric of daily life. Co-founder of Shepherd's Heart Ministries International and ordained minister, Arlene lives in Florida with Jim, her husband of 40+ years, three daughters, and eight grandchildren. Her work invites you to notice the God who's been revealing Himself in your story all along.

LET'S STAY CONNECTED

This book might be ending, but our conversation doesn't have to. I'd love to walk with you as you continue your own journey of encountering God, discovering love, and experiencing transformation.

Visit My Website

You'll find more stories, reflections, and resources for your spiritual growth journey at:

arlenecook.com

Join Me on Social Media

I share everyday moments where God shows up, reflections on growth and healing, and the ongoing story of encountering God in the ordinary.

Follow me on:

Linktree:	Linktr.ee/arlenemcook
Instagram:	@arlenecookauthor
Facebook:	www.facebook.com/arlene.cook.9210

Explore Arlene's Photography

Arlene's passion for capturing beauty extends beyond words. Her photography—featuring serene seascapes and nature's quiet gifts—invites you to pause and experience God's whispers in the everyday. Visit her website at **www.arlenecook.com** to view her work, where select pieces are available for purchase.

YOUR STORY MATTERS TOO!

If this book touched your heart, would you take a moment to share your story?

Leave a Review

Your honest review helps others find these stories when they need them most. Whether it's a single sentence or a longer reflection, your words matter.

- **Amazon:** Search for "Encounter God: When Ordinary Moments Reveal Extraordinary Love" by Arlene Mancilla Cook

- **Goodreads:** Share what resonated with you

- **Your own social media:** Tag me @arlenecookauthor so I can celebrate with you

Tell Me Directly

I read every message. Seriously. If a particular story touched you, if you had a breakthrough moment while reading, if you just want to say hello—reach out through my website or social media. Nothing brings me more joy than hearing how God is moving in your life.

Share With Someone Who Needs It

You probably know someone who's wrestling with wrong images of God, carrying wounds from their past, or hungry for authentic transformation. Maybe this book could be the conversation starter they need. Sometimes the most powerful review is simply saying to a friend: "This book helped me. I think it might help you too."

Your journey of encountering God doesn't end with the last page of this book. It's just the beginning. And I'd be honored to be part of your story as you walk forward into all the love, healing, and transformation God has waiting for you.

With love and expectation for all God is doing in your life,

Arlene

"Encounter God, Encounter Love, Encounter Transformation"

www.ingramcontent.com/pod-product-compliance
Lightning Source LLC
Chambersburg PA
CBHW051505150726
47997CB00001B/117